SHAKER WOODENWARE

A Field Guide

VOLUME 1

SHAKER WOODENWARE
A Field Guide
VOLUME 1

By June Sprigg and Jim Johnson

PHOTOGRAPHS BY
PAUL ROCHELEAU

BERKSHIRE HOUSE
GREAT BARRINGTON,
MASSACHUSETTS

SHAKER WOODENWARE: A Field Guide, Volume I
Copyright © 1991 by June Sprigg and Jim Johnson. All
photographs, except pages 28, 36, 42, 44, and 45, copyright
© 1991 by Paul Rocheleau. All rights reserved. No portion of
this book may be reproduced — mechanically, electronically,
or by any other means, including photcopying — without
written permission of the publisher. For information address
Berkshire House, Publishers, Box 915, Gt. Barrington, MA 01230

ISSN 1053-13X
ISBN 0-936399-06-6 (paper)   /3.00

Printed in the United States of America
10 9 8 7 6 5 4 3 2 1

FIELD GUIDES TO
COLLECTING SHAKER ANTIQUES

Shaker Woodenware, Vol. I — Boxes, carriers, buckets, dippers, sieves, pails and tubs.

Shaker Woodenware, Vol. II — Woodworking tools, textile tools, kitchen utensils and farm tools.

Shaker Baskets and Poplarware — Mount Lebanon production baskets; Canterbury baskets; baskets from other communities; early and transitional poplarware, and other poplarware.

Shaker Textiles, Costume, and Fancy Goods — Household carpets, coverlets and quilts, towels and bed linens, samplers; costume kerchiefs, gloves and stockings, sweaters and knitted goods, bonnets and hats, cloaks and shawls and fancy goods of the 19th and 20th centuries.

Shaker Paper — Prints and engravings, photographs and stereopticon views, postcards, labels, billheads, advertising and other business paper.

Shaker Iron, Tin, and Brass — Stoves and stove tools, lighting, kitchen utensils, and other metalware.

Shaker Furniture — Production chairs, community chairs; stands and small tables, small cupboards and shelves, beds and cots, and counters and casepieces.

OTHER BOOKS ON SHAKER PUBLISHED BY
BERKSHIRE HOUSE/
BERKSHIRE TRAVELLER PRESS

By Ejner Handberg:
Measured Drawings of Shaker Furniture and Woodenware
Shop Drawings of Shaker Furniture and Woodenware, 3 Vols.
Shop Drawings of Shaker Iron and Tinware

"All work done, or things made in the Church for their own use ought to be faithfully and well done, but plain and without superfluity. All things ought to be made according to their order and use; and all things kept decent and in good order according to their order and use. All things made for sale ought to be well done, and suitable for their use."

— Father Joseph Meacham
First American-born leader
of the Shaker society
(1741-1796)

ON THE COVER

ON A SCALE of 1 to 10, these three oval boxes are all 10s on our list. Size, color, and original finishes make these boxes exceptionally desirable. The large box is prized for its clear, bright yellow stain (a finish that the Shakers evidently liked very much), and for its large size. Collectors whose goal is to put together a colorful stack find that the largest and smallest sizes, harder to find than the in-between boxes, command a premium.

The small moss-green box is desirable for its small size and attractive, unusual color. The other box is a favorite of ours for its unusually high proportions, as well as for the subtle beauty of its red-brown stain.

The boxes are characteristically made of maple and pine, held together with small copper tacks. The largest is 7 ¼ inches by 15 inches by 11 inches. The smallest is 2 inches by 4 ¼ inches by 2 ⅞ inches.

Hancock Shaker Village, Pittsfield, MA

CONTENTS

A NOTE ON THE SHAKERS

The Shakers — or the United Society of Believers in Christ's Second Appearing, as they called themselves — began their history in Manchester, England in the mid-18th century. An illiterate factory worker named Ann Lee, born in 1736, became the leader of the sect.

In 1774, she and eight followers set sail for America, where they believed they could live a more holy life, free from the persecution they experienced in England, and with the hope of establishing a new way of life for themselves and their followers.

Arriving in New York, they eventually traveled north on the Hudson River and settled at Niskayuna, which was also called Watervliet, a few miles from Albany, New York. With her small band of followers, she prepared for converts. She died in 1784, several years before the first Shaker village was established.

In the 1790s, the number of converts began to grow dramatically. By 1800, eleven communities had been formed in New England. In the first years of the 19th century, the Shakers pushed westward and established a community in Pleasant Hill, Kentucky, in 1806. Shortly after, other communities were formed in Kentucky, Ohio and Indiana.

By 1840, there were eighteen communities in existence and the Shaker population peaked at approximately 4,000 to 6,000. Prior to the Civil War, their numbers began to diminish and reached approximately 1,000 by the end of the century. Beginning with the closing of Tyringham, Massachusetts, in 1875, the communities began to dwindle. Today only two survive — Canterbury, New Hampshire, and Sabbathday Lake, Maine.

Shaker belief was practiced in communities where members devoted themselves to work and worship. Believers, as they called themselves, were organized in families of celibate brothers and sisters.

Life within the community was quietly busy. Large communal Families of celibate Brothers and Sisters shared responsibilities equally but worked and slept in separate quarters. There were special houses for children, brought into the community with their families or as charitable wards. Following Mother Ann's dictum, "Put your hands to work and your hearts to God," the society spent every day but the Sabbath at work.

Their main business was raising food and providing daily necessities for family members. But they were also craftsmen in a wide range of trades: carpentry, cabinetmaking, blacksmithing, spinning, and coopering, to name a few.

Shaker craftsmen and craftswomen incorporated their principles into their work: durability, simplicity, utility, perfection, grace. Their religion fostered excellence in temporal as well as spiritual matters. The Shakers recognized talent as a gift from God and believed themselves entrusted to develop their abilities to the highest degree.

Living in community also affected Shaker work. Communal life freed individual members from the economic pressures of life experienced by craftsmen in the world. In such an atmosphere the finest work was expected and accomplished.

Because of the fine craftsmanship and durability of Shaker goods, the number of customers for Shaker-made products in the 19th century was large. Among the products made and sold by the Shakers were many common forms of woodenware — boxes, carriers, sieves, dippers, pails, and other forms.

While the number of Shakers has diminished to fewer than a dozen, interest in their crafts continues to grow. What makes Shaker craftsmanship exceptional is the passion for excellence and the emphasis on simplicity. The work of the Shakers continues to be admired and respected. The objects they made represent the essence of Shaker life: utility combined with simple grace. In the objects they made, their spirit and standards for perfection of workmanship live on.

INTRODUCTION

I N THE PAST DECADE, appreciation for Shaker design has increased enormously. The useful, everyday objects that Shakers made are more and more prized for their simple beauty and superior workmanship.

Unfortunately, enthusiasm has spread more quickly than information. While there are reference books on a variety of Shaker products, including chairs, baskets, textiles, and furniture, there has not been, until now, a comprehensive guide to identifying small wooden objects. As a result, there is a great deal of confusion about what is Shaker and what is not.

Recently, at a large group antiques shop in New Hampshire, about two dozen buckets and firkins were offered for sale from $75 to $185. The highest priced example, a green firkin, was called Shaker. It had nice old paint, but it wasn't Shaker. The lowest priced example, which was stuffed into the bottom of a booth, was really Shaker, but it was not sold as such. Even with some repairs, it made a nice buy at $75.

Collectors sometimes pay more than they should for something that is not what it is said to be. The confusion and frustration that result are discouraging. Another problem is that the waters of research and knowledge are constantly being muddied. Researchers have to wade through a swamp of questions to know whether an object is really part of the puzzle, or just something being misrepresented. Finally, the confusion diminishes the achievement of the Shakers, who produced genuinely beautiful and well-made objects. The second-rate, poorly made country woodenware — in some cases, from who even knows what country — offered as "Shaker" only diminishes the Shakers' real achievements.

This book is our attempt to make more widely known

much of the information that has been, to date, common knowledge to a small number of collectors, dealers, curators, scholars, and research-minded craftspeople. It is a book to take along when you go antiquing. We have tried to make it, above all, a practical book. It is not intended to be a scholarly study. It is a guidebook to help you evaluate the woodenware that is sold as "Shaker" at flea markets, at auctions, and in dealers' shops.

Please remember that every type of object in this book was also made by non-Shakers. The key to Shaker manufacture lies in the details, not in the general form. Our hope is that the large, clear photos and the descriptive captions will draw your eye to the specific features that identify Shaker work.

In choosing the illustrations, we have sought to include a representative range of examples, some very common, some more rare, and one or two that may be one of a kind. We do not think everything in this book is equally desirable or equally beautiful. Both of us tend to like the colorful paints and more robust details (like handles) of early-to-mid-19th-century Shaker work, rather than the more delicate, natural wood items made in the late 19th century. We do, however, believe that everything in the book is genuinely Shaker, except where we clearly indicate otherwise in the final section of questions and answers for collectors.

We ask two questions whenever we see a piece of woodenware that is called "Shaker": 1) Is it real? 2) How good is it on a scale of 1 to 10? We have not included any objects that we would rate under a 7 in this book, because we believe the collector should buy only quality objects.

Here are the characteristics that we look for in determining the quality of a piece; the more of these characteristics, the higher the number:
- a beautiful form;
- original finish, especially original paint or stain;
- excellent condition — no repairs or recent changes;
- excellent provenance — bought directly from the Shakers, or can be traced directly back to Shaker ownership;

- an inscription, especially name or date —
  the earlier, the better.

We have organized our discussion of specific types of woodenware into four sections: boxes and carriers, dippers, sieves, and pails and tubs. At the beginning of each section will be basic information about that particular type of Shaker woodenware, including a little history about where it was made and dates of manufacture. We also briefly describe how it was made and what to look for when trying to authenticate it.

For specific information on the various forms of Shaker woodenware, see the pictures following the general intro- duction in each section. Here will be tips to help you identify details of construction and design features, and other infor- mation needed to authenticate a true Shaker object. This section also includes some of the terms used by specialists to describe the construction and parts of woodenware.

The number of illustrations in each chapter is not in proportion to the number of objects that exist in that category. Because Shaker boxes are so readily identifiable and also so well known, we have included only a small sampling. We have not included many dippers or sieves because not that many exist in museum collections, nor do many turn up in the market each year. We have included many pails, on the other hand, because they have the most variety, little about them has been previously published, and there is more confusion about what is a Shaker pail and what is not, than in the other categories.

We are grateful to the people who helped make this book possible. We thank the staff at Hancock Shaker Village, Pittsfield, Massachusetts, and the Shaker Museum, Old Chatham, New York. Jerry Grant was particularly helpful. As always, it was a joy to work with Paul Rocheleau, whose photographs inevitably capture the essence of each object.

Several dealers and collectors made their collections available to us, and we thank them all. We are particularly grateful to Steve and Miriam Miller, who went to exceptional lengths to help us get the photographs we wanted, and to Bob Hamilton, who sent us fine photographs by Greg Heisey.

Color Plates

1. **Two Nests of Oval Boxes**

New Lebanon, New York
(Largest, right) Height: 5 ¹/₂ inches Length: 13 ¹/₂ inches Width: 9 ¹/₂ inches
Maple sides, pine bottoms, copper tacks and points
Hancock Shaker Village, Pittsfield, Massachusetts, 62-28, 64-207, 64-236

2. **Dippers**

New York or New England; Mid-19th century
Length: 7 ¹/₂ inches; Unidentified wood
Hancock Shaker Village, Pittsfield, Massachusetts, 64-9 and 66-171
(The pail is described on p. 98)

3. **Two Tubs**

Probably New Lebanon, New York; Early to mid-19th century
Pine staves and bottoms, iron hoops

(Front) Height to rim: 14 inches
Height of back: 21 1/2 inches
Diameter, top: 19 3/4 inches
Diameter, bottom: 18 inches
Hancock Shaker Village,
Pittsfield, Massachusetts, 63-566

(Back) Height to rim: 13 inches
Height of back: 21 inches
Diameter, top: 17 3/4 inches
Diameter, bottom: 16 inches
Private Collection

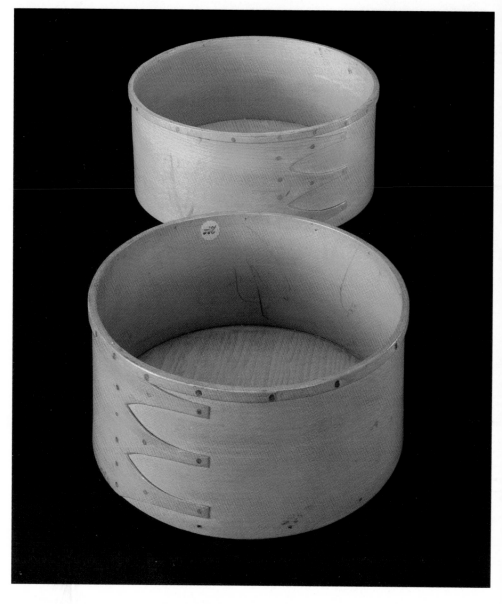

4. **Two Spitboxes**

New York or New England; Mid-19th century
Height: 3 1/4 inches
Diameter: 7 1/2 inches and 7 7/8 inches
Maple sides and rim, pine bottoms, copper tacks and points
Hancock Shaker Village, Pittsfield, Massachusetts,
L65-16a and b

5. Lidded Pail

New Hampshire; Mid-19th century
Height to rim: 10 3/4 inches
Diameter, top: 12 3/4 inches
Pine staves and bottom, birch handle, apple knob, iron bail and hoops
The Shaker Museum, Old Chatham, New York, 6353

6. **Tub**

Probably New Lebanon, New York; Mid-19th century
Height to rim: 16^1/$_2$ inches
Height including handle: 21^1/$_4$ inches Diameter, bottom: 27^1/$_4$ inches
The Shaker Museum,
Old Chatham, New York, 12,824
(The pail is described on p. 128)

7. Two Pails

New Lebanon, New York; Early to mid-19th century
(Right) Height to rim: 7⁷/₈ inches
Height of "ears": 1³/₄ inches
Diameter, top: 10¹/₄ inches
Diameter, bottom: 9 inches
Pine staves and bottom, ash handles, ash and iron hoops, hardwood pins
Hancock Shaker Village, Pittsfield, Massachusetts, 80-27 and 62-460.1
(The pail on the left is described on p. 125)

1

Boxes
and
Carriers

O F ALL THE PRODUCTS made by Shakers, none is lovelier or more familiar than the oval wooden box with finger or "swallowtail" joints. Shaker oval box-making began as early as the 1790s at New Lebanon, New York, making it one of the earliest Shaker industries. The craft continued until about World War II, with the work of Elder Delmer Wilson (1873-1961) of Sabbathday Lake, Maine, the last Shaker oval box maker. The Shakers made oval boxes in production quantities in several communities, including New Lebanon, New York; Enfield and Canterbury, New Hampshire; Alfred and Sabbathday Lake, Maine; and Union Village, Ohio.

The Shakers were not the first to make this type of box, which had a long history in Europe and early America, nor were they the only makers of such boxes in 19th-century America. They refined and perfected the boxes to such a degree, however, that Shaker examples are easily recognizable when you know what details characterize Shaker manufacture.

Look for a pleasing elliptical shape. The oval shapes of most non-Shaker boxes are different — elongated, pointy, formed of two circles joined by arcs, and so forth. Why are Shaker boxes oval rather than round? We don't know for sure, but several reasons seem to make sense. An oval shape fits better in the hands; it's easier to grasp the lid to take it off. An oval box fits better on a narrow shelf. You don't need as wide a board to make the tops and bottoms.

Also look for a snugly fitted top and bottom. The ends of the sides should taper so that the overlap is hardly thicker than the side itself. With a few exceptions, the sides are made of maple. The lids and bottoms are made of high-quality pine that is characteristically tightly grained and free of flaws.

Look for a pleasingly curved "Gothic" arch formed between the fingers (like the shape of the pointed arches in Gothic cathedrals). The fingers most often point to the right as you look at the box. The edges of the fingers are almost always chamferred, that is, cut at an angle with a knife, rather than sawn at a right angle. Look also for tacks that form neatly aligned rows up the side of the box, as straight as a row of buttons. The tacks are usually copper, but the Shakers also used iron tacks, especially on some boxes that seem to be earlier. The bottom is attached to the sides with tiny copper or iron tacks called "points."

In general, the Shakers stained or painted most of their oval boxes in solid colors up until the Civil War. Boxes made after that were more commonly varnished, rather than painted or stained. In the late 19th century, the Shakers occasionally applied a coat of varnish over an earlier stain. Since the Shakers sold many oval boxes, it's not always possible to know whether the Shakers or a worldly owner applied the paint. There are so many old painted boxes that were acquired directly from the Shakers in the 20th century, however, that we have a reasonable idea of the most common Shaker colors. Dark red and bright yellow were characteristic. Blues and greens, which tend to be considered more desirable, are less common but still well represented. Judging from Shaker furniture, interior woodwork, and wooden items in general, the Shakers preferred thin paints and transparent stains that did not conceal the grain of the wood. There are some Shaker boxes with decorative old painting or graining, but those are not typical, and were probably almost all painted by non-Shaker owners.

Today, the most highly prized boxes are either very large or very small (to round out a stack), or have their original paint or colored stain. The largest boxes we have seen are about 2 feet long — the smallest, about 2 inches. Many Shaker oval boxes are marked in ink or pencil with names, initials, dates, and sometimes contents. Not all names are Shaker, however, since worldly buyers also signed the boxes they owned.

(Continued on Page 31)

8. **Oval Box**

Probably New Lebanon, New York
Height: 3 7/16 inches   Length: 9 inches   Width: 6 1/8 inches
Collection of Bob Hamilton

The oval box on page 28 is the only one we have seen with dividers. Those and the nice old inscription make it special. Otherwise, the materials and construction are characteristic of Shaker oval boxes.

a. *Maple sides and lid rim*
Maple bends readily without cracking when soaked or steamed, so it was the standard choice for oval box sides.

b. *Fingers or "swallowtails"*
Note how the edges are chamferred or beveled — i.e., trimmed with a knife at an angle along the sides and at the tips. Note also the nicely proportioned Gothic arch between the fingers.

c. *Copper tacks*
Note how the tacks form straight vertical lines. Time usually darkens the copper so it may look like iron, but a closer look will show the copper's color. The absence of rust marks around the tacks usually indicates that they are copper.

d. *Pine lid*
The pine used in Shaker lids and bottoms is typically of very fine quality, tight grain with close growth rings. Lids and bottoms were characteristically made of pine. This grain is unusually coarse. This is a good example of the characteristic Shaker oval box shape.

e. *Pine bottom*

f. *Iron points*
Shaker boxmakers used tiny wood, iron, or copper points to hold the sides and lid rim to the top and bottom. These are copper. There is no glue in Shaker boxes — the points and tacks in the fingers do the job. It is not unusual for a point or two to be missing. Unless so many have fallen out that the box is in danger of coming apart, it's usually not considered a problem.

g. *Inside*
The inside of the box should always look relatively fresh, light in color, and new, because it was protected from light, air, and dust. If it doesn't, it's probably been oiled or stained and has lost its original surface. The inside end of the box sides is characteristically planed to almost paper thinness, so that the side of the box is scarcely thicker where it overlaps than where it is a single layer. The pine dividers interlock into each other's slots.

h. *Inscription*
The orientation of the word "Spice" is of interest. When you read the word right-side-up, the finger is on the back of the lid, suggesting that it was not intended to be seen. What we consider the front of oval boxes — the side with the fingers — may have been regarded as the back by Shakers and others in the early to mid-19th century.

9. Oval Box

New Lebanon,
New York
Mid-19th century
Height: 5 ¹/₂ inches
Length: 13 ¹/₂ inches
Width: 9 inches
Maple, pine lid and bottom,
copper tacks, points
Collection of
Fran and Herb Kramer

One of the keys to Shaker manufacture is the way the fingers lie flat on the side of the box. Hold the box on its side and look down the length of the fingers. On a Shaker box, the entire finger should be tight against the side, and the tip should not gap away from the side. Many reproduction Shaker boxes have fingers that don't lie as flat.

(Continued from page 27)

"Left-handed" boxes, on which the fingers point to the left as you look at the box, are less common than right-handed boxes, but are not more desirable because of that. In fact, some people who want to build a stack prefer all right-handed boxes for a more uniform look.

The Shakers also made round boxes with fingers, although these are less common. We have seen many, many non-Shaker round boxes with straight seams, usually referred to as "pantry boxes." There are a few that are definitely Shaker, but they are so scarce that we have not included any examples in this book, to avoid confusion.

By adding a handle to a box, the Shakers created the carrier, another woodenware form. The Shakers made them in a number of styles and sizes. Oval carriers are more common than round or rectangular examples. Oval carriers were made by the Shakers in several communities throughout the 19th century and well into the 20th century. In general, early carriers (made before the Civil War) have a dry stain or paint, usually dull red or yellow, and a gracefully carved, fixed handle. Carriers made later have a shiny, clear finish over a light-colored wood, and simple, flat handles that swing.

Oval carriers came in a wide variety of sizes, from about 5 to 15 inches long. Most are about 9 to 12 inches in length.

If you can identify an oval Shaker box, you won't have any trouble identifying an oval Shaker carrier, but look at the handles carefully to distinguish early rectangular carriers. The carved handle is the key. The graceful narrowing of the fixed handle just above the body, swelling back out as the handle rises, is a characteristic to look for. Other makers used bentwood handles, but we have seen the graceful carved shaping only on early Shaker work. The handle extends all the way down the side of the carrier to the base. Handles may be attached on the inside or the outside. Most handles are on the outside, which makes a more pleasing design since the line of the handle does not disappear inside the carrier.

In the late 19th and early 20th century, the Shakers produced large numbers of oval sewing carriers lined with silk and fitted with sewing accessories. They were a popular item in Shaker gift shops and an important income-producer. A well-known self-portrait photograph of Elder Delmer Wilson of Sabbathday Lake, taken in the 1920s, shows him in front of 1,083 recently finished carriers, probably a record production.

The Shakers also made rectangular carriers, usually of maple or pine with an ash handle, although these are much less common. The more desirable carriers are dovetailed together; others are simply nailed. The characteristics of finish and handle type mentioned above are true of rectangular carriers as well.

These Shaker carriers represent a variety of shapes. On all of them, however, the beautifully shaped handles are the visual key to Shaker manufacture. They were all made in New York or New England in the early 19th century. The carrier at right was made at New Lebanon, New York.

(LEFT TO RIGHT)

10. **Round Carrier**

Height: 10 1/2 inches
Diameter: 14 1/2 inches
Ash sides and rim, pine bottom,
hickory handle, iron tacks,
dark red stain
Hancock Shaker Village,
Pittsfield, Massachusetts
62-459

11. **Rectangular Carrier**

Height: 15 inches
Length: 19 7/8 inches
Width: 10 1/4 inches
Pine sides and bottom,
ash handle, copper tacks,
yellow stain
Hancock Shaker Village,
Pittsfield, Massachusetts, 62-18

12. **Rectangular Carrier**

Height: 10 1/4 inches
Length: 13 3/8 inches
Width: 11 1/2 inches
Pine sides and bottom, hickory handle,
copper tacks, dark red stain
Collection of Suzanne Courcier and Robert W. Wilkins

13. Oval Box

Possibly Harvard or Shirley, Massachusetts
Mid-19th century
Height: 4 ¹/₈ inches   Length: 11 ¹/₄ inches   Width: 8 ¹/₈ inches
Maple sides, pine lid and bottom, copper tacks
Hancock Shaker Village,
Pittsfield, Massachusetts, L65-12f

This box was originally painted a warm orange-red, since faded to a muted brown with a decidedly pinkish cast. Traces of the original color can be seen where it has not been exposed to sunlight and dirt.

Typically, the box was painted with the lid on. If the area under the rim is painted, it usually indicates a later repaint. Bottoms of boxes were not usually painted, but occasionally we see a box with its original paint that also has the original color on the bottom.

Inscriptions and markings on boxes are fairly common. They usually designate ownership or use. There were at least two Shakers named John Robinson, whose name is written in ink on the inside of the lid. One died in the Church Family at Enfield, New Hampshire, in 1841 at age 26. The other stayed at Watervliet, New York, for just over a year in 1831-32.

According to museum records, this box was part of a group of boxes acquired at Harvard or Shirley, Massachusetts, early in the 20th century.

a. *Fingers*

The maple that forms the oval sides is exceptionally thick. The fingers are also unusually thick because the maker did not taper them towards the tips. Instead, he cut boldly chamferred edges on the sides of the fingers, which contribute to the appeal of this box. However, the finger on the lid is tapered, and the chamferring is less pronounced. The maple that forms the lid rim is thinner than the box sides.

b. *Lid*

The lid fits snugly. If you turn the box over, the lid remains securely in position. This box has stood the test of time very well.

c. *Copper tacks*

The arrangement of copper tacks is typical. There are two tacks at the base of each finger, one at the center, and one at the end. If the tacks on a box do not follow this characteristic pattern, it is possible that one or more has been added at a later date.

CHAPTER 1

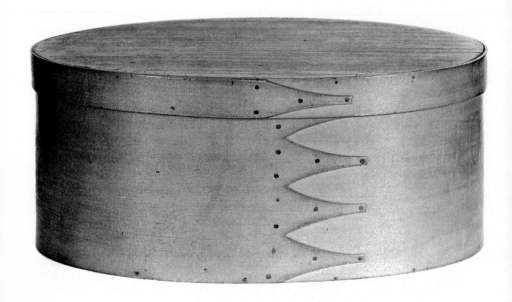

14. **Oval Box**

New Lebanon, New York
Circa 1828
Height: 6 ³/₁₆ inches   Length: 14 ⁷/₈ inches   Width: 11 inches
Maple sides, pine top and bottom, ochre stain, copper tacks
Collection of Bob Hamilton

Oval boxes were made at New Lebanon since at least 1798. The inscription on the paper label on this box suggests it was made no later than 1828 and perhaps earlier.

When attempting to date New Lebanon boxes, it is helpful to know that in 1832, the Shakers at New Lebanon introduced a planing machine for use in making the sides of oval boxes. Boxes made at New Lebanon after 1832 bear the marks of this machine.

a. *Inscription*
Written on a paper label glued to the inside of this beautifully crafted box is the inscription (in ink) "Betsy Bates./ Febr 1828." Betsy Bates (1798-1869) came to the Shakers as a teenager and eventually served in New Lebanon's Parent Ministry, the highest Shaker authority. She was 30 when she received

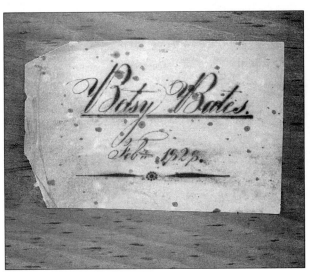

this box. The design element under the signature indicates some skill in decoration. It consists of an ornamental device composed of a circle formed with small dots between two flaring horizontal lines. This simple and quaint device is similar to some of the decorative elements in many Shaker spirit or "gift" drawings.

Also written in ink on the side of the box are the words "Bonnet Trimmings."

b. *Fingers*
Oval boxes of this size usually have five fingers, or swallowtails. However, we have seen at least one box of similar size with six.

15. Large Oval Box

Church Family, New Lebanon, New York
Early to mid-19th century
Height: 7 1/4 inches   Length: 23 1/8 inches   Width: 12 5/8 inches
Maple sides, pine lid and bottom, copper tacks
The Shaker Museum, Old Chatham, New York, 4158

This box is distinguished by its remarkably large size and elongated oval shape. At nearly 2 feet in length, it is one of the largest Shaker oval boxes known. It is relatively narrow for its length.

This box was once finished with a soft orange wash which was later removed, perhaps by the Shakers in the early 20th century when it was fashionable to strip the painted surfaces of furniture and other wooden objects. The color is still visible on the side of the box under the rim, since whoever removed the paint did not bother to take the top of the box off during the process.

The box was acquired from a woman whose father lived for many years as a Shaker at New Lebanon.

a. *Scribe line*
Shaker box makers sometimes drew or scribed a line on the side of the box to line up the fingers. The vertical scribe line is still visible at the point of the arches on the side of this box.

b. *Old repair*
Probably because of the extremely elongated form of the box, the wood at both ends is split at the top of the box. These inch-long splits were repaired with small copper tacks driven through the split from the outside and clinched over on

the inside of the box. These tacks seem to be the same age as other tacks in the box, and were probably put there soon after the box was made. The tendency of the maple side to split when bent too sharply at the end of the box is probably the reason for the rarity of this form.

c. *Fingers*

The fingers on this box are long and slender — just what you would expect on this Modigliani-style box. The Gothic arch between the fingers is quite compressed, in keeping with the elongated proportions of the box.

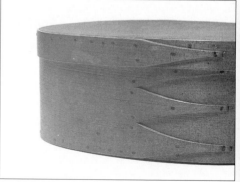

16. Oval Box

New York or New England
Early to mid-19th century
Height: 3 ³/₈ inches   Length: 9 ¹/₂ inches   Width: 7 inches
Maple sides, pine lid and bottom, copper tacks, wooden pins
The Shaker Museum, Old Chatham, New York, 16,047

This box is a variation of the typical Shaker oval box, distinguished by its more squared oval shape and tucked fingers. Boxes of this type are rare. There is some evidence that oval boxes like this were made by the Shakers, so we have included this example in the book, but be aware that it is not yet known whether the Shakers made these boxes or not.

a. *Tucked fingers*
The end of each finger is tucked into the side of the box through a tiny hole. On the inside, the ends of the fingers appear as small wooden points of a different color, flush with the inside surface.

The fingers on this box are very slender and unusually long, almost 3 inches. The ratio of the overall length of the box to the length of the fingers is nearly 3:1. A typical box-to-finger ratio is approximately 5:1.

b. *Wooden pins*
Almost all Shaker boxes are held together with copper or iron tacks, but this box was assembled using tiny, rectangular wooden pins. The only metal fasteners used on this box are four small copper tacks — one at the end of each finger, just before it tucks into the side of the box.

c. *Finish*
Most Shaker boxes were painted or varnished on the outside to protect the wood from dirt and wear. However, many boxes never had a finish of any kind. This box is an example. The maple sides have darkened to a nice, warm brown, and the pine top is darker still from age and the accumulation of dust and dirt.

We rarely see Shaker boxes and carriers with painted decoration. The Shakers considered ornamentation unnecessary and eliminated it almost entirely from their work. The flowers were probably painted by non-Shaker owners in the 19th century. The original color of the thinly painted design has faded to a medium brown color.

The most interesting thing about the decoration is its placement on the box, on the side opposite the fingers. This suggests that the fingers were regarded as the back of the box. Today, the fingers are regarded as the front, but we continue to see boxes on which the placement of the decoration or inscriptions indicates that the fingers were not intended to be seen.

17. Oval Box

Sabbathday Lake, Maine
Early 20th century
Height: 2 $^3/_8$ inches   Length: 6 $^{15}/_{16}$ inches   Depth: 4 $^3/_{16}$ inches
Maple sides and top, pine bottom, copper tacks and points
Collection of Bob Hamilton

This is a fine example of the oval boxes made by Elder Delmer Wilson (1873-1961) at Sabbathday Lake, Maine. Delmer Wilson was the last Shaker to make oval boxes and carriers. He also made some pieces of furniture still in use by the Shakers at Sabbathday Lake.

While these boxes are finely made, they differ from most other Shaker oval boxes in several respects: the shape is a long, slim oval — more elongated than the typical Shaker oval box; the fingers are closer to the end of the box than on most oval boxes; they are closer together; the tacks at the base of the fingers are evenly spaced down the side of the box, and not "paired" as on many other Shaker oval boxes. The box is covered with a clear varnish which is typical of late 19th-century and 20th-century oval boxes.

a. Sides

Although Delmer Wilson made some boxes with cherry sides, the sides and top of this box are figured maple. The use of figured maple in oval boxes is not uncommon, but is usually found on 20th-century examples.

b. Inscription

Written in pencil on the bottom are the words "Presented to our nurse/ Miss Jennie Comery,/from her friend/Delmer C. Wilson/Christ-mas." This inscription is believed to have been done in December 1913 when Jennie Comery visited Sabbathday Lake to treat three sick members of the community.

18. Oval Box

Sabbathday Lake, Maine
Early 20th century
Height: 3 ¹/₁₆ inches   Length: 8 ³/₁₆ inches   Depth: 5 ¹/₂ inches
Gum top and sides, pine bottom, copper tacks and points
Collection of Bob Hamilton

This box made by Delmer Wilson is notable because the top and sides seem to be made of gumwood. The use of gumwood for this box probably indicates it was made as an experiment or as a special gift.

Like other Delmer Wilson boxes, this one has a long, slim oval shape and is finely constructed.

a. *Inscriptions*

— Written in pencil on the inside of the lid is "Presented to/Eldress Lizzie Noyes/December 25, 1906/ From Delmer."

— Written in ink on paper label on the bottom: "Made and presented to/Lizzie Noyes by Delmar Wilson/ of the Shaker Society at/Sabbathday Lake, Maine. She in/turn presented it to Mary A/Wilson of E. Canterbury, N.H." This label was written by Marguerite Frost (1892-1971) of Canterbury, who served the community as teacher, nurse, eldress, theologian, and historian. "Delmar" is a variant spelling.

19. Round Tray

New York or New England, possibly Sabbathday Lake, Maine
Early to mid-19th century
Height: 2 1/4 inches   Diameter: 8 1/2 inches
Maple sides, pine bottom, copper tacks and points
Private Collection

The Shakers made round boxes with fingers, although oval shapes are much more common. This small round container is similar in size and shape to spitboxes (see page 20), but it lacks the characteristic thin rim at the top edge. The fingers are unusually delicate.

a. *Finish*
The warm brick-red color is rich but transparent, revealing the grain of the wood underneath — an effect the Shakers evidently liked, judging from many examples of furniture, interior woodwork, and wooden items. The stain covers the entire tray, including the bottom — a relatively rare finishing touch. The colored stain was topped by a clear finish, either varnish or shellac, for a bit of gloss, but only on the outside surface, not inside or on the bottom. The glossy finish is very old but we are not certain if it was part of the original look or a somewhat later alteration.

b. *Inside end*
Typically, the interior end tapers to a paper-thin edge. The top corner is trimmed at an angle to help eliminate the possibility of its catching on something and breaking.

c. *Inscription*
Written in pencil on the underside is "Sabbathday Lake, Maine." It is important to learn to recognize genuine, old inscriptions. We have seen many faked inscriptions on Shaker (and non-Shaker) items on the market, some more skillful than others. Obviously, ballpoint pen and Magic Marker are not genuinely old! If you look at enough examples of 19th-century handwriting, you can usually tell what's real and what's not.

20. Oval Carrier

New York or New England
Mid- to late 19th century
Height: 3 1/2 inches   Length: 11 inches   Width: 7 3/4 inches
Maple sides, pine bottom, ash handle, copper tacks
Hancock Shaker Village, Pittsfield, Massachusetts, 68-70

This carrier is "left-handed" — that is, the fingers point to the left. (Construction of a left-handed form is simple. The bottom was simply fit into what would be the top of a right-handed piece.) Left-handed carriers are even more rare than left-handed boxes, since fewer carriers were made. However, left-handed boxes and carriers are not more valuable because of their rarity.

a. Handle
The handle is most unusual. It does not extend to the bottom of the carrier, but instead terminates about ¼ inch above the bottom in a rounded end. The handle is thin and finely shaped.

b. Tacks
Note how the copper tacks are not lined up in a straight row. This carelessness is unusual in Shaker boxes and carriers. The tacks are different from the tacks used on most other Shaker boxes and carriers. Their heads are domed, not flat, and round, not slightly oblong. The bottom is attached with the same kind of tacks, not with the standard tiny points.

c. Finish
The transparent, rust-colored stain covers the entire carrier, including the inside and the bottom.

21. Oval Carrier

New York or New England
Mid-19th century
Height to rim: 3 7/8 inches   Height of handle: 9 1/4 inches
Length: 13 inches   Width: 9 1/2 inches
Maple sides, pine bottom, ash handle, copper tacks and points
Hancock Shaker Village, Pittsfield, Massachusetts, 85-203

This carrier is a little larger than usual. The fixed handle is attached to the inside. Outside handles are more common on surviving examples, and we generally think they are more pleasing because the line of the handle is not interrupted.

The finish is not entirely original and not particularly attractive. It appears this carrier was originally varnished, but that strong cleaning removed much of the varnish finish, especially on the ends of the fingers. The spaces between the fingers are much too clean. On an original untouched surface there should be a natural darkening at the point where the fingers come together from the accumulation of dust and dirt over the years. The inside was not left in its natural dry state, but has been oiled, giving it an unpleasant color and appearance.

Another clue is the natural wear that results from years of handling. (If you are uncertain about where to look, pick the carrier up as if you are using it to help determine where most of the wear should be on the sides and handle.) The wear on this carrier is far too uniform to be the result of daily usage.

a. *Handle*
The handle becomes slightly flatter inside the carrier, probably so it will not interfere with the contents (not a consideration, of course, when the handle is attached outside). It is unusually thin over all, and does not exhibit the graceful curves from thick to thin that can be found on handles of more "classic" carriers.

The best thing about the handle is the inscription "PHY" burned into the top. This may designate a location — perhaps "pharmacy" — or it may represent a Shaker's initials.

b. *Tacks and points*
The inside seam is fastened by two copper tacks, driven from the inside and clipped flush outside. The overlap is reinforced by the copper tacks which hold the handle in place. They are likewise driven from the inside, and appear as tiny dots on the outside. The bottom is attached with copper points about 2 inches apart. One that protrudes a little is visible on the right edge. It is not uncommon for points to stick out a little or fall out entirely as the wood changes over time.

22. Lidded Carrier

New York or New England; Early to mid-19th century
Height to top of lid: 3 ¹/₂ inches   Height of handle: 10 inches
Length: 15 inches   Width: 10 ⁵/₈ inches
Maple sides, pine lid and bottom, ash handle, copper tacks and points, iron nails
Hancock Shaker Village, Pittsfield, Massachusetts, 62-21

Covered carriers with fixed handles are very uncommon. Perhaps this is due to the fact they are somewhat awkward to use. The lid has to be slid out under the handle when it is removed or replaced.

The carrier is also made interesting by the height of the handle, nearly twice the height of the sides. The unusual proportions add to its appeal.

The handle is slightly asymmetrical due to shrinkage. Lopsided handles are not desirable, but it's usually best to leave them as they are. We know of one restorer who was asked to straighten a handle that had gone badly askew. He wisely declined on the basis that it might do more harm than good.

The carrier was formerly owned by Faith and Edward Deming Andrews, who published it in plate 34 of *Shaker Furniture* (1937) .

a. *Handle*

The handle is similar to Shaker basket handles, with a flat top and a gently rounded underside. There are slightly angled wood shims on the side of the carrier where the handle is attached to allow space so that the lid can be fitted in place. Note how the right end of the handle was cut to follow the angle of the bottom finger on the side, and how the left end was trimmed to match. Most fixed handles were simply cut straight along the bottom.

The handle is attached with copper tacks like those used to assemble the box. However, at some point, the handle must have become loose, and two iron nails were added to secure it to the side.

When we first looked at this handle, we thought it was a very old addition to a lidded box, but upon close examination, we found that the copper tacks attaching the handle and on the box had identical age characteristics, and we decided that the handle was part of the original design.

b. *Lid*

The top is separated slightly from the rim due to shrinkage. Wood shrinks because the cells loose moisture with time. Wood that is well dried before use shrinks less than green wood. When the top pulls away from the rim some of the points attaching the top to the rim become loose and fall out, as they have on this carrier.

c. *Top*

The top is nicely darkened as a result of dust and dirt settling on it over the years. The top should be darker than the sides on a good, untouched example. Don't try to clean it to make the color more uniform — you'll be spoiling a natural sign of age.

23. Lidded Carrier

New York or New England
Mid-19th century
Height: 7 inches   Length: 15 inches   Width: 11 inches
Maple sides, pine lid and bottom, ash handle, copper tacks and points
Hancock Shaker Village, Pittsfield, Massachusetts, 71-338

This type of handle is very unusual on Shaker carriers. We know of only two or three examples like these. The swing handle is held in place by a straight dowel, fastened on the outside with a wooden pin.

The maker attached a vertical upright to the outside of the box to provide a support for the handle. This narrow piece of maple shims the handle out from the box so that the lid can easily fit over the top. It is trimmed on the bottom to correspond with the curve of the bottom finger. The handle and the uprights are beautifully formed, with a great deal of labor and care evident in the carved shaping.

a. *Fingers*

This carrier has five fingers on the side and one on the lid. We would call this a five-fingered box, but as they say about counting fingers, "It's five if you're buying, and six if you're selling." Boxes with four, five, or six fingers are highly desirable and usually have nice height and pleasing proportions.

b. *Lid*

The lid is a different color from the sides, but it's lighter, not darker as it should be. In addition, it has no gradations in the color that come from age and handling. Alas, in cleaning it years ago to make it look "better," someone removed part of its value and appeal.

c. *Insect damage*

There are small insect holes in the pine bottom and in the handle, probably the work of powder post beetles. Powder post beetles are the scourge of museums and collectors since they can destroy a wooden object in a short period of time.

Some beginning collectors see these holes as a sign of true age. But more experienced collectors know that they are a warning sign that there may be serious damage beneath the surface. We would hesitate to acquire any object with this kind of damage, especially if the holes are new (look for a light color and bits of sawdust). For treatment, contact a professional conservator who specializes in objects made of wood. Museums in your area can help you find conservators.

24. Oval Carrier

Sabbathday Lake, Maine; Early to mid-20th century
Height to rim: 2 ³/₈ inches   Height including handle: 5 ¹/₂ inches
Length: 7 inches   Width: 4 ⁵/₈ inches
Cherry (?) sides and handle, pine bottom, copper tacks and washers, iron rivets
Hancock Shaker Village, Pittsfield, Massachusetts, 66-169

Oval carriers of this type are the last examples of woodenware made by the Shakers. Elder Delmer Wilson (1873–1961) of Sabbathday Lake made thousands of carriers in the early 20th century. For some years near the end of Elder Delmer's life, oval carriers made by a friend and neighbor, Gus Schwerdtfeger, were stamped with the Sabbathday Lake mark and sold in the gift shop. Few people can now tell the difference. We don't know who made this carrier.

While these late carriers are beautifully made, they are different from carriers made a century earlier. The biggest difference is in the handles — thin, flat strips with rounded ends, attached with rivets so they can swing up for carrying and down for use. These late handles do not have the robust carved shaping of earlier handles.

Another difference is the finish — not a colored wash, but a colorless varnish that emphasizes the natural grain of the wood. This finish reflects the general American preference for natural wood in the late 19th and 20th centuries, which the Shakers shared. The bottom is finished underneath, an uncommon feature on 19th-century boxes.

a. Cherry sides

It is rare to see a wood other than maple used for oval box sides, but cherry also lends itself to bending. Elder Delmer Wilson and Gus Schwerdtfeger both made boxes out of cherry and other woods. Note that the inside seam is not tacked from the inside at the top as on most earlier Shaker boxes, but is held in place by pressure alone.

b. Fingers

The fingers are much closer to the end than is typical on other oval boxes and carriers. On most Shaker work, the fingers would be barely visible from this perspective.

c. Handle

The handle is attached with a brass rivet and three copper washers — one inside the box, one outside the handle, and one between the handle and the outside of the box, to give the handle room to swing. Note, too, how the inside ends of the handle are tapered to keep them from rubbing the box when the handle is moved.

d. Sabbathday Lake stamp

25. Sewing Carrier

(Top)
Alfred, Maine
Late 19th or early 20th century
Height to rim: 3 ¼ inches   Height including handle: 7 ⅝ inches
Length: 10 ¾ inches Width: 7 ¾ inches
Maple sides, pine bottom, copper tacks, brass rivet, silver-gray satin lining,
ivory satin ribbons
The Miller Collection

(Bottom)
Sabbathday Lake, Maine
Early to mid-20th century
Height to rim: 2 ¾ inches Height with handle: 6 inches
Length: 8 inches Width: 5 ¼ inches
Oak sides, pine bottom, copper tacks and rivet, iron points,
rosebud print fabric lining
The Miller Collection

Sewing carriers were a joint effort of Shaker Brothers and Sisters. The men made the carriers, which were finished, lined, and filled with sewing notions by the women. This distinctively Shaker product was a popular gift item through most of the first half of the 20th century.

These two very nice examples are stamped with Shaker marks and in excellent condition. It's rare to find carriers in like-new condition because the satin lining and ribbons are so susceptible to damage from use, light, and dust. Collectors should be careful to look for replaced parts — the entire lining, one or more of the sewing notions, or a ribbon or two. Look for signs of age in the satin, check to see that all the ribbons match, and look carefully at each accessory. All four standard accessories are available as high-quality reproductions today, and some craftspeople specialize in refitting sewing carriers.

a. Sewing accessories

Both carriers have the standard equipment: pincushion, wax cake, emery, and needlebook. Clockwise from upper left in the larger carrier are: a poplar-cloth needle book, edged with white kid; a fluted wax cake in its original tissue paper wrapping; an emery-filled strawberry, for cleaning and sharpening needles; and a square pincushion.

In the smaller carrier are the standard tomato-shaped pincushion, a cylindrical wax cake, a felt needlebook, and a strawberry emery. A word about the needlebooks: poplarware was a craft unique to the Shakers, who split and wove thin strips of poplar wood into a "cloth" used to cover sewing notions and boxes. The substitution of felt for poplar-cloth in the needlebook in the smaller carrier undoubtedly has to do with its later date. By this time, the poplar-cloth industry had faded away. The use of printed fabric lining is late and uncommon. Satin in solid colors is the norm.

Note how each accessory is tied to the carrier with a satin ribbon finished in a bow outside. If an unlined carrier has four pairs of small holes drilled in the sides, it has lost its lining and contents.

b. Tacks and points

The older, larger carrier has the usual, somewhat oblong, flat-headed copper tacks and points.

The tacks on the fingers are uncharacteristically crooked and a little irregularly spaced in relation to the fingers. Note that this carrier is "left-handed" — the fingers point left. The smaller, later carrier has round, dome-headed copper tacks and round-headed iron points, not the earlier rectangular points. The use of oak rather than maple for the sides is unusual, although 20th-century Shaker oval boxes and carriers have more variety in the wood than those made in the 19th century.

c. Handles

The ends of the handle on the larger carrier are simply rounded, not chamferred or tapered. Both handles are what we call "popsicle stick" or "tongue depressor" handles — thin, flat strips of wood, bent into a curve, lacking the carving and shaping of earlier 19th-century work.

d. Alfred, Maine, stamp

(On bottom of larger carrier.)

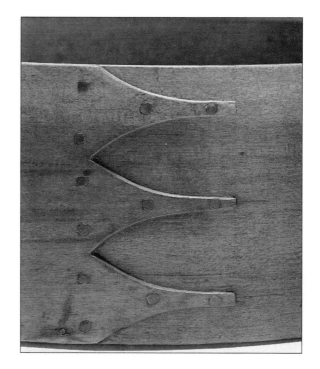

26. **Oval Box**

New York or
New England
Early to mid-19th century
Height: 3 ¹/₂ inches
Length: 9 inches
Width: 6 inches
Maple sides, pine lid
and bottom,
copper tacks, iron points
Collection of Jerry Grant

A few oval boxes have these distinctive, sharply tapering fingers. The fingers are 1 ¼ inches at their widest point, but quickly taper to a width of ⅛ inch about halfway down their length.

A second characteristic feature of these boxes is the slight rounding of the top edge. This rounded edge is extremely unusual — the top edges of almost all Shaker box sides are flat.

Another unusual feature of these boxes is the depth of the rim on the lid (not shown). Although the overall height of this box is only 3 ½ inches, the rim is a full 1 inch in width.

There is some evidence for attributing these boxes to a maker in Canterbury, New Hampshire, but it is possible they were made at New Lebanon for a brief period of time. They probably date to the first half of the 19th century.

27. **Round Lidded Carrier**

New York or New England
Mid- to late 19th century
Height to rim: 5 inches   Height including handle: 9¼ inches   Diameter: 9 inches
Maple sides, pine lid and bottom, ash handle, copper tacks and points
The Miller Collection

This is the only round lidded carrier that we have seen to date. In basic form, it is like the unlidded round boxes with fingers used as "spit boxes" or spittoons, but its sides are higher. The maker added a lid and a handle to make a carrier that was probably a novelty in its own day.

This container was probably used in a dwelling or a Sisters' shop. It has the fine appearance we associate with objects produced for light household use. It is also possible that it was made for sale, but if so, it was evidently not produced in large numbers. It is said to have come from a house in Harvard, Massachusetts.

a. *Handle*
The ends of the handle are unusual because they were rounded by sanding on both sides to form a sharp knife edge. We have not seen another handle end shaped in this way. The carved shaping of the uprights is especially crisp and pleasing.

The maker used copper rivets to attach the handle and added a copper spacer between the handle and the side of the carrier to allow the lid to fit without rubbing the handle.

b. *Inscription*
Written in pencil on the bottom is "$5.00." It was either the cost when new or, more likely, the Shakers' price to a worldly antiques collector earlier in this century.

28. Round Carrier

Probably Harvard, Massachusetts
Mid- to late 19th century
Height to rim: 3 ¹/₂ inches   Height including handle: 7 inches   Diameter: 6 inches
Maple sides, pine bottom, ash handle, copper tacks, iron points
The Miller Collection

The body of this straight-seamed carrier is exactly like a Shaker dipper (or dry measure) in its construction. The difference is that the maker added a high arched handle. This unusual form is one of only a few we have seen. Because of its rarity, we believe it was made for use in the Shaker community, and not mass-produced for sale.

a. *Handle*

The handle goes straight to the bottom on the inside of the carrier. It is fastened with copper tacks driven through the handle from the inside.

The beauty of this piece, and the clue to Shaker manufacture, is the line of the handle. It is like Shaker basket handles, squared in profile, with sharply angled corners from which the handle descends in a straight line. The handle itself is flat on the outside edge and gently rounded inside.

b. *Tacks*

The color and surface quality of the tacks can help tell us whether an object has been refinished or not. On an "untouched" object, the color of the copper has usually become dull with age.

c. *Inscription*

Written in pencil on the bottom is "25c," probably the Shakers' price to an antiques collector early in this century. There is also an old paper tag tied to the handle, with this inscription in ink: "This was made by the Harvard Shakers — came to me through the Albrights — could go to the Shaker Museum in Harvard."

Although it's easy to fake a label, it's difficult to do it well enough to deceive anyone with some experience in looking. This label is genuine, and its information is probably accurate. The Harvard Shaker community closed in 1918. Some of its furnishings were shipped to the Shakers in Sabbathday Lake, Maine, and others were sold. The "Shaker Museum in Harvard" undoubtedly means the Fruitlands Museums, established in 1914 by Clara Endicott Sears, which included one of the earliest Shaker museum collections in existence.

29. Square Carrier

New York or New England
Mid-19th century
Height to rim: 4 ³/₄ inches   Height to top of handle: 9 ¹/₂ inches
Length: 10 ¹/₂ inches   Width: 10 ¹/₂ inches
Pine sides, dividers, and bottom, ash handle, iron tacks and screws
Private Collection

We have seen many divided wooden carriers with fixed handles on the market that are called "Shaker." Large numbers of these carriers were made in the 19th century because they were so practical for use in the shop and home. However, true Shaker examples are rare.

Most Shaker straight-sided carriers are rectangular. This one is unusual because it is square.

a. *Sides*

The sides are dovetailed at the corners. Traces of dark red color remain in the dovetails, indicating the carrier was originally painted.

Sometimes we hear that an object is Shaker "because it's dovetailed," or that it's not Shaker "because it's not dovetailed." Neither generalization is true. Shaker craftsmen often did make fine dovetailed joints, but so did other worldly makers. We have also seen Shaker pieces with crude dovetails, or simple nailed joints. The main point is that we can expect to see high-quality dovetailing on most of the best Shaker work, but it doesn't make sense to call something Shaker or not Shaker on the basis of dovetailing alone.

b. *Handle*

A better indicator of Shaker manufacture is the handle, which has the typical squared profile with sharply curved corners where the handle descends to meet the sides. The handle is attached with large old iron screws (one on the outside, one on the inside) which were too long for the job. They have been trimmed off with a file where they protrude through the opposite side.

30. Three Rectangular Carriers

(Top)
New York or New England
Late 19th century
Height to rim: 3 ¹/₈ inches
Height including handle: 6 ⁷/₈ inches
Length: 8 inches   Width: 5 inches
Butternut sides and bottom, ash handle, copper rivet, iron nails
Hancock Shaker Village,
Pittsfield, Massachusetts, L65-83

(Center)
New York or New England
Mid- to late 19th century
Height to rim: 3 inches
Height including handle: 7 ³/₈ inches
Length: 8 inches   Width: 5 inches
Butternut sides and bottom, ash handle, copper tacks
The Miller Collection

(Bottom)
New York or New England
Mid- to late 19th century
Height to rim: 2 ¹/₄ inches
Height including handle: 5 ¹/₄ inches
Length: 5 ¹/₂ inches   Width: 3 ¹/₂ inches
Butternut sides and bottom, ash handle, copper tacks
The Miller Collection

Like oval carriers, rectangular carriers come in a variety of sizes with either fixed or swing handles.

The swing-handle carrier, top, was evidently intended to be used as a sewing carrier. There are two small holes on each side and both ends where sewing accessories would have been tied with ribbons. However, there is no evidence that it was ever completed for use as a sewing carrier.

The applied bottom extends about $\frac{1}{16}$ inch beyond the sides of the carrier. It is attached with tiny iron nails driven up through the bottom into the sides. The carrier has an old varnish finish inside and out. The sides are quite thin and the dovetails are extremely fine, giving the carrier a very delicate appearance.

The two fixed-handle carriers are made from heavier stock and the dovetail joints are significantly larger than on the first example. The larger of these two carriers is also drilled for the addition of sewing accessories, although the holes are much closer together on this carrier — about $\frac{3}{8}$ inches apart, compared with a $1\frac{3}{4}$–inch space between holes on the swing-handle example. Unlike the swing-handle carrier, the fixed-handle carriers are not varnished inside.

The top edges and corners of all three carriers are slightly rounded. At first we thought this might be the result of sanding during refinishing, but since at least one of these carriers clearly has its original surface, it was probably done when the carriers were made.

a. *Handles*

The swing handle is attached with a small copper rivet which is simply clinched over on the inside to hold the handle in place. The handle ends are rounded and chamferred.

The fixed handle on the smaller carrier is attached with two round-headed copper tacks clinched over on the inside. The end of the handle has been trimmed to a V on which the tip has been clipped squarely off. The sides of the clipped V are nicely chamferred. The extended length of the fixed handles down the sides of the carriers is more pleasing to us than the short swing handle.

It is not known where these small, delicate carriers were made. But in the extreme delicacy of their dovetails, the thinness of the sides and bottoms, and use of butternut, they relate to other Shaker work from Canterbury, New Hampshire, and Enfield, Connecticut.

2

Dippers

THE SHAKERS MADE two types of dippers. One type consists of a round body with a turned handle attached to the body with a rivet. The second type is smaller and is carved from a single piece of wood.

Dippers with turned handles were made in large numbers and in many sizes, which were available for sale in nests.

This type of dipper was made of maple or ash that was soaked or steamed and then bent around a mold for shaping. The sides are joined with a straight seam, not with finger joints as on oval boxes. The seam is fastened with copper tacks, closely spaced (about ⅛ inch apart) to keep the edge from buckling. A bottom of thin pine was fitted and attached with small copper tacks driven through the sides into the bottom. The turned handle is maple and is attached to the body of the dipper by a large rivet at the base of the handle.

Dippers were designed principally for measuring portions of dry substances such as grain or flour and were used in both the household and in trade.

It is important to remember that there were many manufacturers of wooden dippers in addition to the Shakers. Most of the dippers on the market today were not made by the Shakers but by one of the many other manufacturers of woodenware in the 19th century.

Some Shaker dippers have the initials "DM" impressed into the bottom. They stand for David Meacham (1744-1826), a senior trustee in charge of sales at New Lebanon, New York. His initials, which came to stand as a trademark for Shaker manufacture, continued to be used for some years after his death. The "DM" mark is the most commonly found of the various trustees' initials that the Shakers used to identify Shaker-made products. We have also seen it on spinning wheels, pails, and herb and seed packages.

The majority of Shaker dippers are not marked. However, they are not difficult to identify, if you pay close attention to the seam and the handle. Here are some tips to help identify a true Shaker dipper:

- Shaker handles are long, slender, and graceful, not chunky or angular like many others we have seen. There is often a single scribe line at the widest point of the handle.
- Look at the seam on the side of the dipper. The edge should be straight and the seam tight. The row of tacks should be absolutely straight and evenly spaced.
- The sides of a Shaker dipper are thin, and it has an overall light appearance. Many dippers sold as Shaker are heavy and crudely formed. Most non-Shaker dippers can be spotted simply from the heaviness of their sides.

31. Dipper

New Lebanon, New York
Mid-19th century
Height to rim: 2 ³/₄ inches
Length of handle: 7 ⁵/₈ inches
Diameter: 4 ⁵/₈ inches Maple sides,
pine bottom, maple or birch handle,
iron rivet, copper tacks and points
The Miller Collection

This is one of the nicest Shaker dippers we have seen. The initials "DM", for David Meacham, are impressed into the bottom.

a. *Inscriptions*
The letters "DM" are considerably larger than we have seen on other examples — ⁷/₈ inch long overall, and ³/₈ inch high. There is a small diamond shape between the two letters.

Written in ink on the bottom is "Made at Lebanon NY./by Shakers." This is the genuinely old kind of inscription that was added by someone who wanted to preserve something of its history.

The small blue paper auction tag scotch-taped to the bottom has "Jordan/Auction" written in pencil. When a marking of some kind preserves the history of ownership, we think it's wise to leave it on. The Shaker objects owned by George and Gladys Jordan, auctioned in Concord, New Hampshire, in 1968, comprised a fine early collection.

b. *Handle*
Many handles on Shaker objects are marked by one or two scribe lines at their widest point, but this handle is not.

c. *Seam*
The sides of the dipper were wrapped around a mold for shaping and fastened with closely spaced copper tacks (eleven on this example). In addition, four tacks are driven through the side from the inside to fasten the inside seam.

d. *Finish*
The dipper has never had a finish of any kind.

32. Large Dipper

New Lebanon, New York
Mid-19th century
Height to rim: 3 ⁷/₈ inches Diameter: 7 ¹/₄ inches Length of handle: 10 inches
Maple handle, beech sides, pine bottom, iron rivet, copper tacks and points
Hancock Shaker Village, Pittsfield, Massachusetts, 66-143

Dippers were made in different sizes. The smaller dipper is very similar to the preceding example, but lacks the "DM" stamp.

In addition to being beautifully made, these dippers are also satisfying to the hand. Pick up a Shaker dipper and you will see how pleasing it can be to use a well-designed object. The Shakers were exceptionally skilled at scaling successful designs up and down, changing sizes — of products like dippers, chairs, cloaks, and oval boxes — without ruining proportions.

a. *Handle*

There is a nice play between the round form of the side and the gracefully elongated shaft of the handle that is both dramatic and simple. There are many non-Shaker dippers called Shaker in the market, but none have handles as graceful as these.

The handle is joined to the box at the overlap of the seam where the box is strongest and where the handle can help to secure the joint. It is attached with a single large iron rivet at the base of the handle. The exposed head of the rivet is about ⅜ inch in diameter and perfectly round. There is clearly a lot of labor and care in the way the rivet was filed to conform to the curve of the handle where it emerges.

The handle of the small dipper is circumscribed by a single scribe line at its widest point. Scribe lines were occasionally used by Shakers as a very restrained decorative feature, often with two or three together. This single decorative element has an enduring and quiet appeal. The handle is joined to the box with a square-headed rivet, not rounded as in the larger example.

b. *Seams*

The inside seam is neatly joined with five copper tacks about ¼ inch from the end of the seam. The outside seam is gently feathered (not chamferred) which makes for a smooth joint where the surfaces join. The pine bottom is attached to the sides with copper points.

c. *Bottom*

The pine bottom is pulling away from the sides due to shrinkage.

d. *Seams*

The inside edge of the seam is feathered, and the top corner is clipped as on oval boxes to prevent its catching and breaking. It is joined to the side with three evenly spread tacks about ¼ inch from the end.

e. *Bottom*

The bottom of the box is made of fine, closely grained pine which was thoroughly dried before it was cut to form the circular bottom. The joint between the sides and bottom on this dipper is still as tight as the day it was made.

33. Carved Dipper

New York or New England
Mid-19th century
Height: 3 ¹/₂ inches Length: 7 inches Diameter: 3 ³/₄ inches
Unidentified wood
Collection of Fran and Herb Kramer

There are not many carved dippers like this, and little is known about their specific histories, but they appear in several important early Shaker collections, including that of Faith and Edward Deming Andrews. The beautifully shaped handle is common to them all. Most of the similar dippers we've seen were painted (see page 18). This one, which never had a finish, has the bleached appearance of wood used in dairy work. The Fruitlands Museums in Harvard, Massachusetts, have a lovely nest of three, painted in different colors.

3

Sieves

A LARGE NUMBER OF SIEVES were made and sold by the Shakers beginning in the early years of the 19th century. For a period of over fifty years, sieve-making was an important business along with the manufacture of pails, tubs, boxes, and other products. The Shaker communities in Harvard, Massachusetts, and New Lebanon, New York, made sieves for sale.

A sieve is made of two round wooden rims, one slightly larger than the other. The smaller rim is set into the larger and holds a tightly stretched woven mat made of wire, horsehair, or silk. The two rims (each fastened with iron or copper tacks) are held in place with small wooden pins or copper or iron tacks. Sieve rims were made of a pliable, sturdy wood, usually ash. They were sometimes tinted with a red or reddish-orange wash. We have seen a few Shaker sieves stenciled or painted with the word "Garden." Shaker sieves we have seen range in size from 2 inches to about 2 feet in diameter. The only way we know to positively identify a sieve as Shaker is to compare it with museum examples that have solid histories of Shaker manufacture.

Sieves were used for household purposes such as sifting flour and ground herbs and spices. They were also employed in the seed business and other industries where it was necessary to sift powdered materials like paint pigments and dyes.

34. **Wire Sieve**

New York or New England; Mid-19th century
Height: 4 $^1\!/_2$ inches   Diameter, top: 17 $^1\!/_4$ inches   Diameter, bottom: 18 $^1\!/_8$ inches
Ash rims, iron wire mat, iron tacks
The Shaker Museum, Old Chatham, New York, 13,809

Sieves with wire screen mesh, made to withstand heavy use, tend to hold up better over time than hair or silk sieves.

The charm of this sieve, and a clue to its Shaker origin and use, is the painted inscription "SEED LOFT, No. 10." The Shakers at Mount Lebanon and other communities were well known for their garden seed industry. 19th-century Shakers used the word "loft" to mean an upper floor in a dwelling or workshop. We're not sure about the meaning of "No. 10," but it might plausibly refer to a number in a set, a room number, or the size of the mesh.

a. *Mat*
The mesh is large, $^1\!/_8$ inch, to sift larger kinds of seeds. We have also seen Shaker sieves with copper, rather than iron, mesh.

35. Hair Sieve

New Lebanon, New York
Mid-19th century
Height: 5 ¹/₂ inches   Diameter, top: 14 ³/₈ inches   Diameter, bottom: 15 inches
Ash rims, iron tacks, brown and black horsehair, mat thread binding
The Shaker Museum, Old Chatham, New York, 366

This large horsehair sieve is in as nearly perfect condition as we have seen. It's rare to find sieves in such good condition because the woven mats are so fragile.

Ash, a hardwood with a relatively coarse, open grain, is a tough, flexible wood, particularly well suited for bending — hence its use in splint seats, baskets and bentwood products like sieves. This is standard sieve construction — a woven mat held between two rims, the top fitting snugly in the bottom. As with bentwood containers, generally, the inside end is thinned to a feather edge, held close to the outer rim by pressure and a couple of tacks driven in from the inside and clipped flush with the surface on the outside. The edge of the horsehair mat is neatly bound with a heavy, crisscrossed thread. A small break in the horsehair on this sieve revealed a thin inner core of some kind of woody fiber around which the horsehair is wrapped.

a. *Tacks*
Note how the closely spaced tacks form a crisp, precise line, like a row of buttons, and how the edge of the seam is beveled, or chamferred, to form a smoother seam.

The tendency of iron to "bleed" a dark, oxidized stain into the wood, clearly visible here, shows why the Shakers, who liked things neat and clean, preferred non-staining copper.

Note how the tacks that hold the two rims together are spaced more closely near the edge of the seam.

b. *Horsehair mat*
The horsehair is woven in a twill pattern (twill weave has diagonal lines — look closely at the denim in your jeans for an example). This mesh is very fine, perhaps to sift the tiniest garden seeds, or even finer powdered substances.

36. Two Sieves

New Lebanon, New York; Early to mid-19th century
(Left) Height: 3 $^1/_4$ inches   Diameter, top: 9 $^3/_8$ inches
Diameter, bottom: 9 $^7/_8$ inches   (Right) Height to rim: 3 $^1/_2$ inches
Height of handle: 7 inches from mat   Width of handle: 1 $^3/_8$ inches
Diameter, top: 9 inches   Diameter, bottom: 9 $^5/_8$ inches
Ash rims, horsehair mats, thread binding, iron tacks, wooden pins
Hancock Shaker Village, Pittsfield, Massachusetts, 63-504 and 62-436

The sieve on the left is stamped "DH" for Daniel Hawkins (1781-1873), the leading trustee at New Lebanon's South and Second Families. He was not the maker but the business agent in charge of sales. His initials served as a kind of trademark or guarantee of Shaker manufacture to the buyers — and they still do to collectors.

The sieve on the right is the only one we've seen with a handle, which we have no reason to doubt was part of the sieve when it was made.

The lower edge of the handle is slightly chamferred, beginning about an inch above the rim. The ends taper in thickness where they are joined. Each end is attached with fine tacks — three driven from the outside in a triangle pattern, and two below driven from the inside out.

The rims on both sieves are nice and sturdy, about ⅛ inch thick. Neither sieve ever had a finish. The sieve on the left has a particularly lovely patina, the rich, dry, dark brown color that only comes to unfinished wood with time and exposure to light.

On the left sieve, the end inside is neatly fastened with two iron tacks driven from the inside and trimmed flush on the outside. The inside end of the handled sieve, right, is not tapered to a feather edge, as is more common, but thins only slightly to a crisply chamferred edge.

The upper and lower rims are fastened together with very tiny wooden pins — seven on each sieve. Most of the other Shaker sieves we've seen use iron tacks, instead, like those that fasten each rim into a circle.

a. *Stamped Initials "DH"*

The initials appear faintly on the left sieve on the upper rim a little to the right of the seam. The initials of Daniel Hawkins appear on other New Lebanon products, including brushes and pails (see page 128). We know of only one other sieve marked "DH," but the extreme similarity of the unmarked, handled sieve on the right leads us to conclude that it was made in the same shop around the same time, probably by the same maker.

b. *Seam*

Note the absolute precision of the spacing of the iron tacks. The seam on the left sieve has a fine, crisp chamfer, and a scribe line to show the maker where to line up the tacks. The neatness of the seams is one key to Shaker manufacture.

c. *Patterned mat*

In the left sieve, the mat has a pleasantly subtle pattern in the twill weave — stripes, formed of four lighter-colored hairs, about ½ inch apart. Stripes or plaids in Shaker sieve mats are uncommon and desirable.

The mat in the right sieve, in almost perfect condition, has an even smaller mesh.

37. Miniature Silk Sieves

Probably New Lebanon, New York
Mid-19th century
(Sieve in front)
Height: 1 ³/16 inches Diameter, top: 2 inches
Diameter, bottom: 2 ³/16 inches
Ash and maple rims, silk mats, thread binding, copper tacks
The Shaker Museum, Old Chatham, New York, 8250, 4478, 2140

These are the tiniest, most delicate Shaker sieves we have seen. We call them miniature to denote their extremely small size, but they were not meant as toys. The silk mesh, as sheer as a silk stocking, was used to sift the finest of powders. The sieve in the front has traces of white powder in the pores of the open-grained rims. Sieves with silk mats are generally on the small side, usually no more than about 6 inches in diameter, because of the delicacy of the mesh.

a. *Seams*
Note how the outside ends are chamferred. The thinner the rims are, the less bold the chamfer can be. The top corner of the seam on the sieve standing on edge is clipped slightly, probably to keep the end from catching on something and breaking. The inside end of the sieve in front was fastened with two tacks driven from the inside. The points, trimmed flush with the outside, are hardly visible. On one of the sieves in the rear, there is only one tack inside, at the top, and the bottom corner has lifted slightly.

b. *Pins*
The tacks that fasten each rim into a circle are readily visible on these sieves. Much smaller and harder to spot are the tiny copper pins that join the upper and lower rims.

38. Footed Sieve

Probably New Lebanon, New York
Mid-19th century
Height of body: 3 5/8 inches
Height to rim: 5 inches
Diameter, top: 10 5/16 inches
Diameter, bottom: 10 1/2 inches
Ash rims, black horsehair mat, ash legs,
thread binding, iron tacks, wooden pins
The Shaker Museum, Old Chatham, New York, 11,734

This is the only Shaker sieve we have seen to date with legs. The wood and hardware of the legs are clearly old, but we're not sure if the sieve was made with them or if they were added a short time later.

a. Rims
The rims are unusually sturdy for the sieve's size, about 1/8-inch thick, making the sieve less liable to buckle or warp.

b. Tacks
Note the tacks' configuration on the bottom rim: four tacks along the end seam and three pairs of tacks neatly spaced to the left. (The lower set of tacks on the upper rim is typically concealed by the lower rim.) The rims taper in thickness for a few inches towards the ends, which are crisply chamferred.

c. Legs
Each slim, graceful leg is held in place with a tack outside and a small, old iron screw inside.

d. Mat
The diagonal pattern of the twill weave is visible in this photo.

4

Pails
and
Tubs

ALTHOUGH WE SEE plenty of pails, firkins, piggins, tubs, and churns on the market that are called Shaker, there are very few that we believe are really Shaker. As a general warning, we would hesitate to buy any firkin or churn as Shaker, no matter how well made. We simply haven't seen enough that are unquestionably Shaker to be able to identify a Shaker version of these common forms. Tubs, too, are usually suspect, although there is more solid evidence to go on.

Pails, however, need not confuse the collector. Like oval boxes, pails were a production item for several Shaker communities, including New Lebanon, New York; Hancock, Massachusetts; Enfield and Canterbury, New Hampshire; Alfred, Maine; and Union Village, Ohio.

Because they were made in large quantities, it is possible to recognize the standardized details that identify Shaker work. It is also not too difficult to learn where a particular pail was made, since the coopers in different villages developed their own "signature" preferences in details like the shape of hoops, handles, and bail plates. The illustrations that follow will help you identify several basic types of pails.

First, though, some terminology. Although most people use the word "bucket" today, Shaker records refer to "pails," so that is what we call them. Your dictionary will make no real distinction between the two, so take your pick. A pail is made of upright staves that are held together with hoops either made of wood or metal. The handle, or bail, likewise, is either all wood or wire with a turned wooden handle. The wire bail is fastened to the pail's sides with two bail plates. The staves and bottoms are almost universally pine. Wooden hoops and bails are usually ash, a wood that bends nicely. The wooden handles on wire bails are hardwood, often birch or maple. Iron hardware is the norm.

A tub is usually larger and/or shallower in its proportions than a pail and has two small side handles instead of an overhead bail. The handles are either metal — usually, wrought iron — or are formed by hand-holds cut into a pair of staves that jut above the rim. An outstanding example of a beautifully made and well-documented Shaker tub appears on page 22. It is uncommonly large and retains its original dark mustard paint.

Pails and tubs were almost always painted to protect the soft pine from wetness. Fortunately, most retain their old paint, probably because pails were not considered highly collectible when refinishing was in vogue to make antiques more salable. The most desirable pails will have their original coat of paint and all their original components. Missing or replaced hoops are a common sight, since pails swell and shrink so much with changes in heat and humidity that the hoops often slip down over time. Make sure that the old paint is really the first coat. A truly original layer of paint will always bring a better price. Look also for markings on pails. They moved around the village so much in ordinary use — from the well to the kitchen, out to the berry fields and back, from the barn to the dairy — that it made sense for the Shakers to mark them so they would be returned to their proper place. Room names (like "Kitchen" or "Syrup Storehouse") are relatively common. Names, initials, and numbers, which can be room numbers or dates, are also common. While the inscriptions on oval boxes are most commonly in ink or pencil, the marks on pails are more frequently in paint, probably to make them last longer in wet conditions.

The illustrations that follow will help you to recognize several basic different types of Shaker pails:

a) Pails and tubs made in and stamped Enfield, New Hampshire

b) Other pails from Enfield and Canterbury, New Hampshire

c) Pails from New Lebanon, New York

d) A few less commonly found pails, like tall seed pails, and "fancy" pails made of variegated woods

39. Pail

New York or New England; Mid- to late 19th century
Height to rim: 8 ⁵/₈ inches   Diameter, top: 11 inches   Diameter, bottom: 10 inches
Pine staves and bottom, hardwood handle, iron hoops and wire
Hancock Shaker Village, Pittsfield, Massachusetts, 68-72

Although the Shakers made some all-wooden pails, with wooden hoops and handles, pails with iron hoops and wire bails are much more common. We don't yet know which community or communities made this type of pail, with its distinctive "coffin" bail plates. Museum records indicate several different sources, including New Lebanon, New York, and Canterbury, New Hampshire. However, the construction techniques are not like those on documented Canterbury pails, so we think it's unlikely that they were made there.

a. *Staves*

The staves on this pail are relatively uniform in width, but this is exceptional. Most staves range from 2 inches to 4 inches in width. The staves on Shaker pails are simply butted together, unless they were made at Canterbury or Enfield, New Hampshire, where two types of tongue-and-groove joints were used (see pages 101, 107). The staves were not glued, but were held together by the pressure of the hoops.

b. *Paint*

This pail has wonderful deep blueberry-blue paint (see page 18). The color is very similar to the dark blue paint used on the trim inside Shaker meetinghouses. Most Shaker pails are mustard, brown, or dull red, so this color is rarer and desirable.

The inside is painted ivory. White and ivory are typical colors inside, we suspect for the sake of cleanliness. The paint is nearly all worn away towards the bottom, which you'd expect to see on a pail that was scrubbed repeatedly.

c. *Hoops*

The ends of the iron hoops on Shaker pails are characteristically trimmed to a pleasing shape, either cut to a V or with their corners clipped. Only the pails made at Enfield, New Hampshire, normally have straight-cut hoops. Note, too, the relatively heavy iron in the hoops, much less flimsy than on most non-Shaker pails. The hoops are usually fastened with two rivets, although these hoops just have one. The hoops are characteristically painted to match the pails.

d. *Bail plates*

This type of bail plate, which resembles a coffin in shape, is relatively uncommon on Shaker pails. We have seen about fifteen examples. Each bail plate is attached with two iron rivets and painted to match the pail.

e. *Wire bail*

The wire on Shaker pails is generally a nice, sturdy gauge.

f. *Handle*

Most handles are made of birch or similar hardwoods. The handles have varying shapes, but are characteristically quite simple, with smooth concave or convex curves, either of which fit nicely in the hand. The handles were usually not painted to match the pail, although this one is. There should be signs of use on the handle.

g. *Bottom*

The bottom is unusually high off the ground, $5/8$ inch or so. Pail bottoms are almost always painted, and the original color, unfaded from light and dust, is often readily apparent here.

40. **Two Lidded Pails**

Enfield, New Hampshire; Late 19th century
Pine staves and bottom, hardwood handle, iron hoops, bail plate and wire
(Left) Height to rim: 7 ³/₄ inches Diameter, top: 9 ¹/₂ inches Diameter, bottom: 8 inches
(Right) Height to rim: 9 ³/₄ inches Diameter, top: 12 inches Diameter, bottom: 9 ¹⁵/₁₆ inches
Private Collection

The late 19th- century stamped pails from Enfield, New Hampshire, are the only Shaker pails that are marked with the word "Shakers." They are well made and attractive, although not as carefully made as earlier pails from Enfield and other communities.

Still, they are much nicer than most non-Shaker pails and sap buckets on the market, and wise buys when the finish is original and the condition is excellent and unaltered.

a. *Impressed stamp*

The telltale stamp indicates Enfield Shaker manufacture. The impressed inscription, which is 2 inches long, reads: "NF SHAKERS" over "ENFIELD N.H." "NF" stands for North Family, who ran the operation. We have not yet seen a faked Enfield stamp, but remember — the paint should be old, and the impression should be under the paint.

b. *Tongue-and-groove joints*

The staves are joined with tongue-and-grooves that are rectangular in profile. This kind of joint is not found on pails or tubs made in other Shaker communities, but it is found on many non-Shaker examples.

Sap buckets are the most commonly found Enfield coopered products. We have seen two basic sizes — a taller bucket, with three hoops, and a shorter version (about 9 ⅛ inches high) with only two hoops.

a. *Paint*

The bucket is painted the same dull mustard color inside and out. This color and a drab red were the two characteristic painted finishes on Enfield sap buckets.

b. *Hoops*

The hoops, which are painted like the bucket, are cut straight at the end and fastened with two rivets. The ends are rather carelessly cut, often at an angle and not straight up and down.

c. *Hanger*

Sap buckets have a single iron tab used for hanging the bucket on a sugar maple tree. We have seen two or three shapes on Enfield sap buckets. This shape, cut to an identical simple arc at top and bottom, was quickly cut from a ribbon of sheet iron that was close in width and gauge to the hoop stock. This hanger is attached to the bucket with an iron rivet above two iron nails.

41. Pail

Enfield, New Hampshire
Height to rim: 9 ¹/₈ inches
Diameter, top: 12 ¹/₈ inches
Diameter, bottom: 10 inches
Pine staves and bottom, birch handle, iron hoops, copper bail
The Shaker Museum, Old Chatham, New York, 7003

This stamped Enfield pail has an unusual variation of the bail plate, an elongated vertical diamond that resembles a coffin in shape. The wood of the staves is visible through the thin red paint. It seems unusual that a pail of this ordinary height should have three hoops instead of two. It has the characteristic rectangular tongue-and-groove of Enfield coopered ware.

a. Handle
The handle, which is convex in profile, has a single scribe line in the center. There are three chuck marks from the turning lathe on each end, indicating it was turned as an individual piece. Not all handles were made as single units. Based on a number of examples we've seen with chuck marks on one end only, we believe many handles were turned from a single dowel-shaped piece of birch or maple, and then cut apart.

b. Wire bail
At first glance we thought the wire was iron, but close examination revealed that it was copper, which has oxidized to a flat charcoal-gray color. It must have presented a striking appearance when the pail was new. The use of copper wire is not characteristic of Shaker pails. If you are unsure whether a bail is copper or not, make a tiny scratch with a knife blade or file in an inconspicuous place and you will quickly see the copper color.

c. Bail plates
The "coffin" bail plate is 2 ¾ inches from the top to where it meets the hoop, and 1 inch in width. Each is held in place with two iron rivets. The iron was finished with a shiny black paint or other kind of coating.

d. Stamp
We were especially interested in this particular mark because there are two "N"s in "NF," with one slightly superimposed over the other. This suggests that perhaps each letter in the mark was stamped separately, at least on this pail, although it is more likely that the entire inscription was done with one stamp, and that the "N" was faint and needed a second strike. There are four chuck marks in the pine bottom where it was attached to the lathe when it was turned.

42. Tub

Enfield, New Hampshire
Late 19th century
Height: 12 inches
Diameter, top: 20 ¹/₂ inches
Diameter, bottom: 18 ¹/₄ inches
Pine staves and bottom, birch handles, brass hoop, straps and wire, brass rivets
The Miller Collection

This is the only marked Enfield tub we have seen to date. This example is in pristine condition. A similar tub appears in a 19th-century photograph of Shaker boys at a well in the Enfield community. The photo is reproduced on page 88 in *The Shaker Image* by Elmer R. Pearson et al. We are not sure of the significance of the line about 1 inch below the rim on the outside. It does not seem to indicate that the tub had a lid, however.

a. *Hoops*
The use of brass is most unusual. The hoop ends are not straight, as is the norm on Enfield work, but are cut to a shallow V.

b. *Finish*
As unusual as it is for a coopered item not to have been painted, this tub has its original varnish finish. There is no evidence of old paint, and the tub has not been refinished. We have seen a similar old, clear finish on a very few other marked Enfield pails.

c. *Handles*
The profile of the handles is unusual — straight, with a swell at the center and beveled ends. There is a scribe center at the center. Each brass strap is attached to the tub with two brass rivets.

43. Pail

Canterbury, New Hampshire; Mid-19th century
Height to rim: 6 ³/4 inches   Length, top: 12 ³/4 inches   Width, top: 11 ⁵/8 inches
Pine staves and bottom, birch handle, iron hoops, bail plates, wire
The Shaker Museum, Old Chatham, New York, 8084

This Canterbury pail is noteworthy for two reasons. First, it is slightly oval in shape — the only oval Shaker pail we've ever seen. A painted inscription on the bottom, "SY Foot," indicates that the pail was used to soak feet, and a foot fits better in an oval than a circle. "SY" is an abbreviation the Canterbury Shakers used for Infirmary.

Second, it's stamped "FW" on the bottom. The initials stand for Francis Winkley (1759-1847). Like Daniel Hawkins (page 129) and David Meacham (page 127) of New Lebanon, New York, whose initials also appear on pails, Francis was not the maker, but the deacon who handled sales of his Family's products. We have seen nine or ten pails stamped "FW." Curiously, no two are alike, and all have particular charm.

a. *Bottom*

The characteristic method of joining staves on Canterbury pails, with V-shaped tongue-and-groove joints, is clearly visible in this view. We have seen only one non-Shaker pail with this unusual construction feature.

Note the neat, wide chamfer around the bottom, a feature of some but not all Shaker pails. The initials "FW" impressed into the center of the bottom are hard to see because of a thick second coat of paint. You probably can't easily see the inscription, either, because it was overpainted with the thick gray-green paint. It is visible only when we turn the bottom so that the raised painted letters catch the light. It reads "SY," with "Foot" below it. According to Irene Zieget, a longtime friend of the Canterbury Shakers, "SY" was a Canterbury abbreviation for Infirmary. We have seen the same initials on a number of other items associated with infirmary use at Canterbury.

b. *Paint*

An old second coat of thick gray-green paint covers the original color, a distinctive grayish-pink that we have seen on a number of items from Canterbury. The original paint on some of the woodwork in the old kitchen area of the Church Family Dwelling House is about the same unusual color. The hoops and bail plates are painted to match the pail. Traces of the green paint are also visible on the wire bail. It's unusual for the bail to be painted.

c. *Bail plates*

The bail plates are not the standard Canterbury diamond shapes, but high rectangular tabs. We've seen this variation on one or two other Canterbury pails, including another stamped "FW." The bail plates are probably made of hoop stock, in a $7/8$-inch width. The inside ends are clipped to a V and each bail plate is fastened to the pail with two iron rivets.

d. *Handle*

The handle, concave in profile, has a central scribe line and one about $1/8$ inch from each end. The original finish, an orange shellac, is nicely worn on the underside.

44. Pail

Canterbury or Enfield, New Hampshire;
Mid-19th century
Height to rim: 5 inches
Height including handle: 9 inches
Diameter, top: 7 inches
Diameter, bottom: 6 3/8 inches
Pine staves and bottom, birch handle,
iron hoops, bail plates, and wire
Hancock Shaker Village,
Pittsfield, Massachusetts, 73-245.1.1

Pails like these were made in large numbers by the New Hampshire Shakers. We have seen at least sixty in public and private collections, the largest single type of surviving Shaker pail. They are almost always in excellent condition because they were so well made. Their staves are characteristically tight and sound, and their hoops have rarely loosened.

Some pails of this type are clearly documented to Canterbury, including one signed by Levi Stevens (1781-1867), principal cooper in that community. Others can be traced to Enfield, where coopering was the principal industry. Records show that 4,000 pails and 500 tubs were made there in 1850. Note that the later, stamped Enfield pails differed in construction details. At this time, we know of no way to tell a mid-19-century Enfield pail from a Canterbury pail.

It is easy to identify mid-19th-century New Hampshire Shaker pails because they have three distinctive construction features. If all three of the following features appear on a pail, it is almost certainly from New Hampshire:

- **Diamond-shaped bail plate** – Be careful, however, as a diamond-shaped bail plate alone is no guarantee of Shaker origin! There are many, many non-Shaker pails with this feature. Notice how substantial this bail plate is, however — much less flimsy than non-Shaker examples made of thinner stock.
- **V-shaped hoop ends** – We have not seen a mid-19th-century New Hampshire Shaker pail without this feature. Again, be careful, though, since we have seen non-Shaker pails with their hoop ends clipped to a V.
- **V-shaped tongue-and-groove joints**

Look at the staves where they meet on the top or bottom, and you will readily see the unusual pointed tongues. For an illustration, see the preceding pail.

New Hampshire Shaker pails come in a range of sizes and with a number of variations, including several different types of lids. This is one of the smallest sizes, and is more square in overall proportions than larger sizes, which flare more towards the top.

a. *Handle*
The shape of the handle varies. Most are convex — that is, they swell outward — and have a single scribe line at the center. Others have straight or concave (in-curving) profiles, with the single scribe line.

b. *Finish*
The pail is painted yellow-ochre on the outside, the most common color. Another relatively common color is cinnamon-brown. We have seen a few pails in original color combinations that include yellow outside/red inside, red outside/yellow inside, and dark green outside/red inside. A very few pails are dark blue. White is a common interior color, especially on the yellow pails. The inside of this pail was not painted but has old shellac, perhaps indicating that it was for "nice" use rather than hard work. The hoops are almost always painted to match the pail.

c. *Stave profiles*
The staves taper to a pleasingly slender rim at the top, with an edge that often measures no more than ⅛ inch. The inside curves gracefully outward, but the outside is straight and does not curve in. The bottom of each stave is flat, curving gracefully on the inside under the bottom to a maximum thickness about twice that of the thin top edge.

45. Lidded Pail

Canterbury or Enfield, New Hampshire
Mid- to late 19th century
Height to lid: 6 inches   Height, including handle: 10 inches
Diameter, top: 8 1/4 inches   Diameter, bottom: 7 1/4 inches
Pine staves, lid and bottom, hardwood handle, iron hoops, bail plates and wire
The Miller Collection

The New Hampshire Shakers fitted some small pails with simple lids. Note how the top point of the diamond bail plate was trimmed to accommodate the lid. If you see an unlidded pail with a clipped bail plate, the pail is missing its lid, and is not in its completely original state.

a. Rim and bail plate
On lidded pails, the outside rim is slightly rounded inward. Although the clipped bail plate and in-curving outside rim make it easy to spot a pail minus its lid, it's usually fairly easy to identify any pail that is missing its lid. Note the wear around the outside rim from small movements of the lid over time.

b. Lid
These simple lids are flat pine discs edged with a strip of iron, held in place with small, square-headed iron tacks.

c. Hoops
The iron hoops are clipped to a V at the end — one of the hallmarks of mid-19th-century New Hampshire Shaker pails. The lid rim is similarly trimmed.

d. Handle
This handle is a more unusual variation. Rather than a smooth convex curve, it looks like two cones that meet at the center scribe line.

e. Impressed number
A large number 7, about 1/2 inch high, is impressed into the bottom and the underside of the lid. We do not yet know its significance. We have seen other numbers — 1, 2, 16, 30 — on other small, lidded New Hampshire pails.

46. Pail

Canterbury or Enfield, New Hampshire; Mid-19th century
Height to rim: 8 ¹/₂ inches   Diameter, top: 13 ⁵/₈ inches   Diameter, bottom: 12 ¹/₈ inches
Pine staves, lid and bottom, hardwood handle and knob, iron hoops, bail plates and wire
The Shaker Museum, Old Chatham, New York, 9149

47. Lidded Pail

Canterbury or Enfield, New Hampshire, Mid-19th century
Height to rim: 9 1/2 inches   Diameter, top: 13 inches   Diameter, bottom: 10 7/8 inches
Pine staves, lid, and bottom, hardwood handle, iron hoops, bail plate, and wire
The Shaker Museum, Old Chatham, New York, 3906

These two pails have several things in common. They were both made at Canterbury, they are both marked "WH," probably for Wash House, and the lids on both, while genuine, are not original to these pails. Since both pails were acquired directly from the Canterbury Shakers in the 1950s, the substitutions were probably made by the Shakers themselves, perhaps many years ago. If you find a "married" lid and pail on the market today, however, it's more likely to be a recent match.

The pail on the left (page 112) has a particularly handsome kind of lid, with a turned knob. Lids like this are not as common as the plainer flat lids.

a. *Lid*

The knob is rather decoratively turned for Shaker work. The lid is formed of two thin pine discs joined with iron tacks. The lower disc fits into the top of the pail, and the slightly larger upper disc rests on the lip.

b. *Paint*

The pail is painted a mustard color. The inside was never painted, but has a modern dark brown oily stain.

c. *Bottom and inscription*

The broad parallel marks of hand planing are clearly visible on the bottom, which has a nice bold ½-inch chamfer around the edge.

The letters "W.H." are painted on the bottom. They appear to have been formed with a stencil, although the letters are not solidly painted, but merely outlined with a narrow black line.

The pail on the right (page 113) is of interest because the initials "JK" were stamped into the bottom. These initials probably stand for John or James Kaime of the North Family at Canterbury, New Hampshire. James (1820-1894) served as an elder, as did John (1792-1877). As usual, "JK" was not the maker of the pails, but the business agent who was in charge of sales. We have seen only two pails marked "JK." The pail was acquired from the remaining Canterbury Shakers in 1950.

a. *Paint*
This pail has two coats of paint — a mustard-yellow over a deeper orange. Many pails have had several coats of paint on the inside where wear or water have caused the paint to peel away.

b. *Handle*
The varnished birch handle is slightly concave. There is a scribe line at the center and one at each end. The scribe line on the right spirals off the edge of the handle — evidence of the chisel being held by an unsteady hand.

c. *Hoops*
The top hoop is distinguished by what we think must be a sheet iron manufacturer's mark, "J[. . . . .] AGNALL & SONS." (The inscription is not completely legible.) The letters are formed of tiny raised dots. We have seen this mark on two other New Hampshire Shaker pails.

d. *Lid and inscriptions*
The pine lid is enclosed by a ¾-inch iron rim made from the same stock used for the hoops. The V-shaped end points in the opposite direction from the V of the hoops.

We do not think that this lid and this pail were made for each other, although both are genuine and old.

"WH/7" is stenciled in black on the top of the lid, but the side is marked "WH/1." Further evidence is the rough tapering of the outside top edge of the pail to accommodate the lid, which was slightly too small for the pail before this alteration.

"WH" is a relatively common mark on Shaker pails and probably stands for Wash House, or laundry. The numbers may be room numbers or numbers in a set.

e. *Bottom*
The bottom of the pail was painted a yellow-orange. A second coat of mustard has been painted over the original color. The outside edge of the bottom is strongly chamferred to fit into the slot cut into the staves. About ½ inch of the chamfer is visible.

48. Oatmeal Pail

Canterbury or Enfield, New Hampshire; Mid-19th century
Height to rim: 9 inches   Diameter, top: 11 ⅛ inches
Diameter, bottom: 10 ¼ inches
Pine staves and bottom, birch handle, iron hoops, bail plate, and wire
The Shaker Museum, Old Chatham, New York, 8957

This is one of our favorite pails — a nice pail made terrific by the crisply painted inscription. It also has an extremely atypical oval bail plate, but in our opinion, that is merely a curiosity, not a valuable "rarity."

The Shaker Museum has three other pails similarly painted with "Rice" and "Beans." Oddly enough, while all four of the pails were purchased directly from the Canterbury Shakers, each was bought at a different time. This was acquired in 1957 from Eldress Emma King. Two of the pails have the standard diamond-shaped Canterbury bail plate, but the other has the same atypical oval bail plate.

This photo shows another characteristic feature of New Hampshire pails — the high, handsome arch of the wire bail.

a. Paint

The pail is painted dark yellow-orange, inside and out. Most pails that we've seen were painted a contrasting color on the inside, or else appear to contrast because the inside is not painted.

b. Inscription

The word "Oatmeal" was applied freehand in thin black paint. This leads us to assume that the pail must have once had some kind of cover to keep out bugs and mice.

c. Handle

The handle, which does not have a finish, is slightly concave in profile, one of the three characteristic New Hampshire handle shapes. There is a scribe line in the center and one ⅛ inch from each end. The handle tapers in slightly beyond the scribe lines at the ends.

d. Bail plate

The bail plate is of particular interest because it is one of only two or three raised oval bail plates we've ever seen on documented Shaker pails. Although these pails are the exception that proves the rule, we emphasize — *don't* buy a pail as Shaker because it has a raised oval bail plate! We see them often on non-Shaker pails. The oval is 1 ½ inches long by 1 inch high and has a raised disc in the center. Each bail plate is attached to the pail with a pair of iron rivets. The bail plates were painted the same color as the staves.

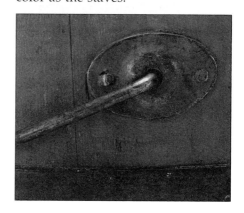

49. Pail

Canterbury or Enfield, New Hampshire
Mid-19th century
Height to rim: 8 ¹/₂ inches
Diameter: 13 inches
Private Collection

Instead of the standard diamond bail plate, a few New Hampshire pails have a bail plate shaped like an inverted teardrop. The original robin's-egg blue paint is crackled and flaking, so it needs to be handled with some care when it is dusted, but the surface is perfectly acceptable and has what one collector we know calls "GHW" — Good Honest Wear.

a. Handle
This handle profile — slightly concave, or in-curving — is found on New Hampshire Shaker pails but is less common than the convex or out-curving profile. Note the three scribe lines — the one in the center is standard, while the two about ⅛ inch from each end are optional. This handle appears to have never had a finish, but other pail handles are often finished with a shiny light-orange stain.

b. Wire bail
The gauge on the wire bails on Shaker pails is generally heavier than that on non-Shaker examples. This results in a sturdy bail that usually retains its original gracefully rounded curve. Note: When the bail is lowered, it should clear the rim and rest on the outside of the pail. If it doesn't, it's probably been replaced.

c. Staves
The staves typically vary in width. On this pail, they range from 2 inches to 4 ½ inches.

50. Syrup Pail

Canterbury or Enfield, New Hampshire
Mid-19th century
Height to rim: 10 ⁵/₈ inches
Diameter, top: 10 inches
Diameter, bottom: 11 ¹/₄ inches
Pine staves and bottom,
birch handle, iron hoops,
bail plate, and wire,
copper pouring lip and tacks
The Shaker Museum,
Old Chatham, New York, 17,511

As we have pointed out, examples of genuine Shaker coopered ware that taper this way—smaller at the top than the bottom—are very scarce. This pail may be one of a kind, since we have never seen another like it. We especially like the sturdy copper pouring lip and the painted inscription underneath, which indicates its use with syrup, probably maple syrup. The Canterbury Shakers maintained an extensive sugarbush and built a large sugar shack to process the sap. Maple sugar and syrup products were an important enterprise well into the 20th century.

The staves are joined with the characteristic New Hampshire V-shaped tongue-and-groove.

a. *Paint*

The dark mustard paint is an old second coat. Underneath is the original coat, a brighter mustard color. Mustard is the most common color on New Hampshire pails of all kinds.

b. *Hoops*

The ends of the iron hoops are as usual clipped to a V and fastened with two iron rivets. The bottom hoop is a nice, generous ⅞ inch in width. It is interesting that the top hoop, which looks slightly less wide, is in fact ⅟₃₂ inch narrower — a subtle proportional adjustment that we think was deliberate. The hoops have both coats of paint. The bottom hoop has been secured to the pail with a few modern copper tacks — evidence of a common problem when the wood shrinks and the once-snug hoop droops.

c. *Bail plates*

The inverted teardrop shape is an uncommon but well-documented alternate to the standard Canterbury diamond-shaped bail plate. Each bail plate is attached to the staves with two copper rivets. The bail plate was painted. It is not possible for us to see if the bail plate ends in a point (concealed under the hoop) or whether the point was clipped off straight to simply butt up against the hoop.

d. *Handle*

The handle is painted dark mustard like the rest of the pail. There is nice wear on the underside, where you would expect it.

The profile is slightly concave, and there are the usual three scribe lines, one in the center, and one about ⅛ inch from each end. The three chuck marks on each end are an unusual feature, showing how the handle was gripped when it was turned on the lathe. Most Shaker pail handles do not show these marks.

e. *Pouring lip*

The heavy gauge copper lip was securely attached to the pail with two rows of copper tacks. It has only the second coat of paint.

f. *Inscription*

The words "Ƨyrup/ƧTH." are painted in black on the bottom. Someone got his "S" backwards. Because "H" was often an initial for "house," and because the Shakers commonly referred to many of their buildings as "houses" — e.g. Dwelling House, Meeting House, Wash House, etc. — we think "STH" may stand for Store House, or a place where syrup supplies were stored.

51. Pail

New Lebanon, New York, or Hancock, Massachusetts
Early 19th century
Height to rim: 9 inches   Height of ear: 2 ¹/4 inches
Diameter, top: 12 ¹/4 inches   Diameter, bottom: 12 inches
Pine staves and bottom, ash handle and hoops, hardwood pins
Hancock Shaker Village, Pittsfield, Massachusetts, 63-539

All-wood Shaker pails are scarce. Iron hoops and wire bail handles are much more common, probably because these features were typical of pails made in the second half of the 19th century. Shaker pails with wooden hoops and handles all seem to come from New Lebanon or Hancock in the first half of the 19th century. A snapshot of a very similar pail was taken by William F. Winter, well known for his photographs of Shaker subjects, at Hancock in 1931.

In spite of everything we've heard about interlocking wooden hoops being "proof" of Shaker manufacture, that is not what our research has shown. While there are a few genuine Shaker items with this feature, we have found that such hoops are far more likely to be a sign of non-Shaker origin.

The real clue to Shaker manufacture here is the handle. We don't mean that all buckets with wooden bail handles are Shaker, but you can, with a little attention, learn to recognize the specific details that identify a Shaker bentwood handle.

a. Handle

The beautifully shaped, labor-intensive handle is the key to this pail's Shaker origin. Note especially these refinements we don't find on non-Shaker bentwood handles:

The outside edge of the handle is flat but the inside is pleasingly curved to fit comfortably in the hand. This shaping is similar to basket handles from New Lebanon, New York.

The handle gets wider and thinner as it nears the pins that hold it to the "ear." The sculptured quality and crisp chamferring of the rounded bottom edge are not typical of non-Shaker handles, which are much more like flat straps.

The top edge of the ear is chamferred towards the inside of the pail. This feature alone is not a guarantee of Shaker make, however. The ear is not just a longer stave — it is almost always carved to the desired width from a particularly wide stave (see how the sides of the stave jut about ¼ inch beyond the ends of the ear).

b. *Paint*

There are two layers of paint, both old. A bright cornflower-blue covers the original pale blue, which remains on the inside of the pail. Neither shade of blue is common on Shaker work.

c. *Hoops*

The chamfers on the edges of the interlocking fingers are much more pronounced than those on the fingers of oval boxes. This is because the wood is thicker. The heavier the stock, the bolder the chamfer can be. Each hoop tapers slightly, from about 1/8 inch at the top edge to about 1/4 inch at the bottom. This construction detail is not distinctively Shaker, however.

d. *Proportions*

Shaker all-wood pails are generally boxier in their proportions than Shaker pails with iron hoops and wire bails. Note how the sides are nearly parallel; there is only 1/4-inch difference between the top and bottom measurements.

52. Pail

New Lebanon, New York
Early to mid-19th century
Height to rim: 7 7/8 inches   Height of ears: 1 3/4 inches
Diameter, top: 10 1/4 inches   Diameter, bottom: 9 inches
Pine staves and bottom, ash handle, hardwood pins, iron hoops
Hancock Shaker Village, Pittsfield, Massachusetts, 80-27

This pail is an unusual and perhaps transitional type. It retains the earlier style of bentwood handle (instead of the typical later 19th-century wire bail) but uses iron, rather than wooden, hoops.

In addition to its pleasing form, the pail has a great original finish — bright mustard yellow paint with a nice dry, unchanged surface — and is documented with the stamped initials "DM."

a. Inscription and bottom
The initials "DM" impressed into the bottom stand for David Meacham (1744-1826), the New Lebanon Shaker business agent who sold, rather than made, these pails. His initials also appear on a dipper in this book (page 77). The large initials "EN." are stenciled in the black paint on the bottom. We do not know their meaning. The bottom is not perfectly flat inside the pail, but is slightly rounded upwards, a feature we have seen on a few Shaker pails and tubs. This gentle swelling is deliberate and not the result of warping, although we are not able to offer any reasons for it.

b. Paint
The pail is painted mustard-yellow outside and white inside, a common interior color in Shaker pails. In this pail, the paint has been entirely scrubbed away about 3 inches below the rim. The "ears" have mustard paint over white on the inside surfaces.

c. Hoops
The hoops are trimmed at the ends to a V whose tip is then clipped a little. The iron rivets which fastened the top hoop are missing, and the old replacements are just nails. There is more rust on the bottom hoop, which seems logical, given that the bottom of the pail is likely to be wet most often.

53. Potty Pail

New Lebanon, New York; Early to mid-19th century
Height to rim: 13 ¹/₄ inches   Height of feet: 3 inches
Diameter, top: 12 inches   Diameter, bottom: 12 ¹/₂ inches
Pine staves, bottom and lid, ash handle, hardwood pins and knob, iron hoops
Hancock Shaker Village, Pittsfield, Massachusetts, 62-76

We have seen four or five Shaker potty pails, all slightly different in their details, but serving the same function — to hold the ceramic pot inside. The wide seat rim and raised height on this pail made it more comfortable to use. The New York State Museum has a potty pail that, according to the Shakers, was made to look like a grain pail to preserve the modesty of the Sisters who carried it to the field or garden for use when returning to the privy was inconvenient.

This example, stamped "DM" for David Meacham (see preceding pail), is the only marked potty pail that we've seen. It is painted mustard, with a brick-red interior.

a. *DM Stamp*
The initials stand for David Meacham (see page 74) and indicate a Shaker origin at New Lebanon.

b. *Iron Hoops*
The corners of the hoop ends are clipped. The top hoop has an old repair — the rivets were replaced and the hoop was re-pierced. The hoop ends point in opposite directions, which is not typical, and the switch probably happened when the top hoop was fixed.

c. *Rim*
The hardwood rim is removable to make it easier to take out the ceramic chamberpot that was once inside. A wooden flange, painted brick-red like the pail's interior, is nailed to the underside of the rim.

d. *Lid*
The lid appears to be formed of two thin discs nailed together, but is actually shaped from a single piece of wood (compare the lid on page 112). The knob is threaded to make it unlikely that it would ever pull out.

54. Pail

New Lebanon, New York
Mid-19th century
Height to rim: 9 inches
Diameter, top: 12 ³/₄ inches
Diameter, bottom: 11 ³/₄ inches
Pine staves and bottom, ash handle, hardwood pins, iron hoops
The Shaker Museum, Old Chatham, New York, 9323

To date, we have seen only three Shaker pails stamped "DH". The initials stand for Daniel Hawkins, (1781-1873), who served as a trustee at New Lebanon's Second Family until 1859, when he became senior elder of the South Family. According to the Shakers' custom, his initials appeared as a kind of trademark or proof of Shaker manufacture on products made for sale in that family. His initials also appear on a sieve (see page 89) in this book.

This pail is as good as they come — marked, excellent condition, handsome details, wonderfully solid construction, attractive color and original thin mustard-yellow paint. It was acquired from a woman whose husband had been raised by the New Lebanon Shakers.

a. *Paint*

The paint is very thin and the wood grain clearly shows through the color — a look the Shakers liked, judging from much of their furniture, interior woodwork, and other wooden products. The inside of the pail is not painted. Curiously, the paint on the pail's bottom is salmon or orange, which is unusual because the paint is usually the same on the sides and bottom. One explanation is that the original color was salmon, which has faded to mustard-yellow, but it doesn't look that way under close inspection.

b. *Hoops*

The iron hoops are a generous ⅞-inch wide — wider than those on many non-Shaker pails, and the stock is nice and thick. The iron was coated with a black shiny finish which looks less like paint than some special finish for metal. Each hoop is fastened with two rivets and has clipped corners. The ends of these hoops point to the left, but other pails' hoops point to the right, so either way seems to have been acceptable. The rivets hold the hoop to itself, not to the pail — pressure alone keeps the hoops in place.

c. *Handle and hardwood pivots*

This is the classic Shaker pail handle — a sign that would indicate Shaker origin even if the pail were not marked "DH." The details in the carving identify this as a Shaker handle (see the three preceding examples). The ends of the handle terminate in graceful arcs, chamferred at the bottom edge. The "neck" above the ear is carefully carved, going smoothly from a

flattened end to a handle that becomes rounded on the inside as it rises. The top surface is flat, and the rounded underside fits comfortably into the hand. The paint on the handle is nicely worn, especially underneath, from being handled.

d. *Proportions*

The pail is unusually square. The taper from top to bottom is only 1 inch. Most Shaker pails flare out at a slightly greater angle.

e. *"Ear"*

Note how the staves that form the raised ears are thicker than the other staves, for greater strength where the handle joins. The top of the ear slants in toward the pail, as do its sides.

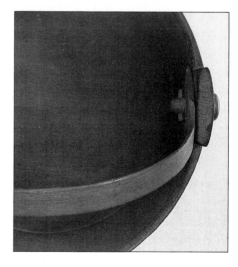

55. Seed Pail

Mount Lebanon, New York
Circa 1874
Height to rim: 14 inches Diameter, top: 15 ¹/₂ inches
Diameter, bottom: 13 ¹/₂ inches
The Shaker Museum, Old Chatham, New York, 9493

We have seen about nine or ten of these late, unusually large pails. Several are dated 1874 and about half are marked to indicate that they were used in the garden. Some have penciled notations that give weights of around 6 to 7 pounds — perhaps pounds of seeds to be sown in the Shakers' vast kitchen or herb gardens or garden seed plots.

a. *Inscription*
Stenciled in black on the bottom is "1874/G," and "6 lbs" is written in pencil.

b. *Finish*
The pail was probably painted dark orange-brown, the usual color on this type of pail. This is not the original surface. There is a newer, thick, shiny finish of either varnish or shellac. It is old enough to have crackled, however.

c. *Hoops*
The hoops were not made with any great care. The middle and bottom hoops, each 1 inch wide, have ends cut in different shapes and pointing in opposite directions. The middle hoop has a straight cut end that points right. The bottom hoop's end, which points left, has lopsided clipped corners. The top hoop may be an old replacement — we can't quite decide. It is narrower than the other hoops, only ⁷/₈-inch wide, and like the bottom hoop, has a clipped corner end that points left. All three hoops are fastened with a pair of iron rivets and painted black.

d. *Handle*
The flat, straplike handle is much less interesting, and required much less work, than the handles in the preceding examples which are much earlier in date. The ash handle is finished like the rest of the pail and is fastened to the staves with hardwood pins, probably maple. The handle is so tight and moves with such difficulty that we wonder if it might be an old replacement.

56. **Striped Pails**

Mount Lebanon, New York; Circa 1875-85
Height to rim: 4 to 5 inches   Height, handle raised: 7 ¹/₄ to 9 ¹/₂ inches
Diameter, top: 6 ¹/₄ to 8 ¹/₄ inches   Diameter, bottom: 5 to 7 inches
Mixed woods, pine or cedar bottoms, hardwood handles,
iron hoops, bail plates, and wire
The Miller Collection

We have seen about a dozen of these small, fancy pails. Although there is some confusion in the records, one is signed by Rufus Crosman (1748-1891), and most or all can probably be attributed to him or to Elder Daniel Boler (1804-1892).

They were made to commemorate the disastrous fire at Mount Lebanon, New York, in 1875. According to several records, the pails were made from the cedar posts of a fence that survived the fire, plus sumac, a very unusual wood for any kind of use.

While the pails are indeed useful as containers, they were clearly intended primarily to be commemorative and decorative, which was typical of much late Victorian Shaker work. These fragile little pails sat decorously on a shelf, not in a sink or dairy.

Surprisingly, these four pails were not acquired as a set, but were found at different times and from different sources by the collector.

a. *Staves*
Pails like this have been called "laminated," but since the staves are not glued together, we don't think that the term makes sense. There is considerable technical expertise in the assembling of all the sliver-like staves. The patterns are all slightly different. Note how the pail in the upper left has a tiger stripe in its light-colored staves. Woe to the collector whose striped pail dries out and falls apart. With some patience, it is possible to reassemble ordinary pails, but we'd hate to have to figure this out!

b. *Handles*
These handles are more decorative than those on earlier, ordinary Shaker pails, both in their turnings and brown pinstriping. We would not be surprised if they were purchased rather than made at home.

c. *Hardware*
The hoops and bail plates are thin iron, painted black. The wire bails look like copper but are actually copper-plated iron, which we have not seen in other Shaker work. The bail plates on the smallest pail are slightly notched on the sides, but all the others we have seen are slender versions of a coffin shape (see page 98.)

d. *Inscription*
The bottom of the smallest pail, which happens to be cedar, not pine, has this pencil inscription: "Marcia/to Alice/Please accept." We can guess that the pail was given by one Shaker Sister to another, some time after it was made, as a token of loving friendship.

57. **Firkin**

New York or New England; Mid-19th century
Height to top of lid: 11 $^7/_8$ inches   Diameter, lid: 12 $^1/_4$ inches
Diameter, bottom: 13 $^1/_4$ inches
Pine staves, lid and bottom, ash handle and lid rim, iron hoops and tacks
Hancock Shaker Village, Pittsfield, Massachusetts, 62-463

We have seen at most a half-dozen firkins in museum collections that we felt sure were Shaker-made. The chances of finding a real Shaker firkin are very, very slim. We thought it was worthwhile to include this genuine example to make that point.

There are two keys to its Shaker manufacture: its excellent provenance and construction details which relate to other, positively documented Shaker products. Faith and Edward Deming Andrews bought it directly from the Shakers sometime in the second quarter of the 20th century. The clipped corners on the hoops, the carved shaping on the handle, and the precise spacing of the nails and chamferred end on the lid rim are all characteristic of Shaker workmanship. The color, a dark red-brown stain, is also something you'd expect on early Shaker woodenware. But remember — it's the combination of all these factors that adds up to a Shaker origin. One or even two of them alone would prove nothing.

By the way, "firkin" is a modern collectors' term for a lidded pail that tapers from wider at bottom to narrower at top — the opposite of a regular pail. It's interesting to speculate why non-Shaker firkins are more common than non-Shaker pails on the market today. We presume it was because firkins, used for dry storage, have lasted longer than pails, which were used in wet conditions and wore out sooner. We can't explain, though, why genuine Shaker firkins are so rare. Perhaps it's because communal Shaker Families used bigger dry-storage containers.

a. *Lid*
The rim is neatly fastened with small rectangular iron tacks and the outside end is crisply chamferred. One small iron nail driven from the inside holds the inner end. The construction of the rim for a round Shaker lid is much like that of a sieve rim. We are not sure what caused the crack in the rim that goes through the seam. It is not an ordinary type of damage and it is likely to have been caused by accidental dropping rather than by a structural stress problem.

b. *Handle*
Note the chamferring and shaping around the curved bottom edge area, that make this handle more appealing than most flat, straplike non-Shaker bentwood handles on firkins.

c. *Inside edge*
The inside of the lip is tapered for about ½ inch. The taper is painted like the firkin, but the rest of the interior was never painted.

58. Tub

New Lebanon, New York
Mid-19th century
Pine staves and bottom, iron hoops, handles, and screws
Height: 8 inches   Diameter, top: 15 ¹/₈ inches   Diameter, bottom: 13 ³/₄ inches
The Shaker Museum, Old Chatham, New York, 4354

We have seen a few Shaker tubs with iron handles. A more common type of handle is the hand-hold cut into two high staves (see page 22). This tub is relatively small in comparison with other Shaker tubs we have examined.

a. *Staves*
The rim has a nice profile. Each stave has a rounded taper up to the ¹/₈-inch flat-top edge.

b. *Paint*
The tub is painted a typical mustard color. It is somewhat lighter in color on the bottom where it has been protected from dust, light, and wear. We have seen other pails that are a different color on the bottom because the pail has been repainted or refinished. Since the raised bottoms don't get much wear, there was usually no need to repaint the bottom too. The color on the bottom usually represents the original color of the object. The inside of the tub was not painted, and the pine has darkened with time.

c. *Handles*
Similar handles were also sometimes used on Shaker furniture, usually blanket chests that were heavy to move when filled. The handles are covered with a shiny black finish.

d. *Hoops*
The hoops are not as nicely made as those on most other Shaker work. The end of the top hoop is V-shaped with the tip trimmed. The end of the bottom hoop simply has the corners clipped.

e. *Bottom*
As on a few other Shaker tubs we have seen, the bottom inside is not perfectly flat, but swells upward in the center. This may be a technique used to give maximum strength to the bottom, but with less weight than if the entire bottom were as thick as its center. This kind of bottom required much more labor to make than an ordinary flat bottom.

5

Questions
and
Answers
for collectors

NOT EVERYONE WHO reads this book will collect Shaker woodenware; some will simply enjoy learning about it. We wrote this section for those who would like to buy something Shaker and for beginning collectors or collectors who would like to improve their skills. As a curator and collector/dealer ourselves, we have had to learn everything we talk about here. We hope that our years of experience can save you some trouble and be of help to you.

1. How can I learn more about Shaker woodenware?

Read about it, look at actual examples, and ask questions. Consult the selected bibliography on page 158. Visit museums with Shaker collections, especially these: Canterbury Shaker Village, Canterbury, New Hampshire; the Fruitlands Museums, Harvard, Massachusetts; Hancock Shaker Village, Pittsfield, Massachusetts; the Metropolitan Museum of Art, New York; the Philadelphia Museum of Art; the Shaker Museum, Old Chatham, New York; the Shaker Museum, Sabbathday Lake, Poland Spring, Maine; Shakertown at Pleasant Hill, Harrodsburg, Kentucky; and Shakertown, South Union, Kentucky.

Talk to museum curators, whose job it is to learn about these things and to share that information. Most curators are happy to answer your questions and to steer you in the right directions. Caution: Don't assume that something was made by the Shakers just because you've seen one on display in a Shaker museum. Be sure to check with the curator. Some objects were owned by the Shakers, but not made by them. Museums with furnished period rooms typically include non-Shaker artifacts. Curators will be able to tell you what they know about the history of objects in their collections. Bear in mind that curators have different areas and levels of expertise and, like everyone else, sometimes make mistakes. Don't hesitate to get several opinions. Remember, though, it's not to a curator's advantage to tell you something is Shaker if it's not, so you can probably get objective opinions from them.

59. Pail

Height: 8 ³/4 inches
Diameter, top: 12 inches
Diameter, bottom: 11 ³/8 inches
Hancock Shaker Village, Pittsfield,
Massachusetts, 89-5

We found this genuine New Hampshire Shaker pail in a group antiques shop in New Hampshire about a year before we started this book.

At $75, it was not only the cheapest pail in the place, it was the only real Shaker example in more than 300 booths. A green firkin that was called Shaker but was not, was the highest priced, at $185.

How did we know it was Shaker, and from New Hampshire? It was a combination of details, all of which we had seen on pails known to have been made at Canterbury or Enfield in the mid-19th century: 1) the distinctive V-shaped tongue-and-groove joint between the staves, most readily visible from the bottom; 2) the hoop ends, trimmed to a V-shaped point; 3) the slightly concave, or in-curving shape of the handle; 4) the cinnamon-colored paint; 5) the overall proportions of height to diameter, angle of flare, and height of body which relates to the painted inscriptions on the two other pails. Interestingly enough, it was the inscription that first said "Shaker" to us in that first split second of examination. The communal Shakers, who technically owned all their possessions in common, and who loved order, were much more apt than ordinary Americans to mark things to make sure they were returned to their rightful places. The initials here probably stand for a place — "WH" may well be wash house, or laundry (see page 113) — and the number may be a set number or a room number.

The top hoop and metal bail plates joining the handle to the body are replacements that are in no way typical of Shaker manufacture. The pail originally had teardrop-shaped bail plates (see page 118).

---

2. Where can I find Shaker woodenware for sale?

Shaker woodenware turns up in antique shops and auctions throughout New England and New York, more often in areas where there were once Shaker communities. If you do a lot of looking, you are sure to run into something Shaker or called Shaker. Ask general dealers who might have some Shaker in their area. They usually know who might have a piece or two. There are very few dealers and auctioneers who specialize in Shaker, but there are many who will have a piece of Shaker now and then. You can also subscribe to the antiques trade papers.

Bear in mind that you should not automatically accept as truth what you see or what you hear. Dealers and auctioneers range from very honest and very knowledgeable to just plain dumb and/or crooked as hell, with every gradation in between. It's sad but true that the antiques field has earned a reputation for "buyer beware." Serious collectors ask around and sooner or later get to know who's reliable and who's not. Don't hesitate to ask questions: "How do you know it's Shaker?" or "What can you tell me about the history of this piece?" Even with the very best dealers, however, the very best collectors ultimately need to use their own judgment.

3. What can I expect to pay?

We decided not to make this book a price guide because the market is too small and too rapidly changing to quote prices that have some basis in reality. Condition is everything, especially original surface. Refinished, repaired, or damaged objects sell for much, much less than their perfect counterparts in original paint. Depending on size and condition, an oval box can sell for as low as $200 to as high as $25,000, the record price to date. Also, the very same object can bring wildly different prices depending on who sells it, where, and to whom. You can expect to pay top dollar at auctions — there's something about the psychology of a public bidding war that sends the prices soaring. As we've often said, if you spend an enormous amount of money in private, there's no audience to applaud and no one will take your picture or print a story on it. These things do happen at auctions, though. Also, buyers who lack confidence like the idea that at least one other person in the group thinks that the object of desire is worth something. This may or may not be true, depending on who's bidding, but the thought is of comfort to many people.

A good way to get an idea of prices is to shop around. Check prices in antiques shops. (By the way, remember that polite haggling is very common in the trade. Don't be afraid to ask "Is that your best price?" You'll often find that there is some reduction.) If a price is not printed in an ad, call the dealer and ask. Call auctioneers to get pre-sale estimates on things in upcoming auctions. Check the antiques trade papers for auction reports, which include prices. Prices paid at auctions are matters of public record, so you can feel free to ask after the fact (although who made the purchase is generally not revealed).

To give you some sense of prices, we can tell you that at an auction in 1989, an oval box sold for $25,000, a record to date. At the same auction, prices for other oval boxes ranged down to $150. Recently, pails have brought $175 to $2,250. We have seen dippers sold for $1,500 and a sieve for $350.

4.   Since original finish is so important, how can I learn to tell the difference between old and new finishes?

We can suggest a few guidelines, but it's really not possible in a book to teach someone how to recognize an original surface. You have to look at objects yourself. The best way to learn is to find someone who can show you what to look for. In the meantime, these tips will at least help you to know what questions to ask. Generally, it's easy to fake an "original" finish, but it's very, very hard to do it well enough to fool an experienced eye.

Old paint is never one uniform color. Chemical and physical changes inevitably produce a wide range of shades. This subtle variation is what makes old paint so pleasing. It is possible to duplicate, but very few take the time or have the skill to do it well. Old paint often has a crackled, irregular surface.

New paint that is altered to look old is something we see all too often. With a few cents' worth of paint and a little time an unscrupulous seller can make a piece look like a great investment, given the market demand for painted woodenware. Some newly painted pieces have brown "antiquing" stain smeared on and wiped off to make them look old, but this method is crude and looks artificial. Some pieces with new paint are artificially "worn" on sides, edges, fingers, and handles, but these, too, are usually easy to spot because it's difficult to make it look natural. Your best tool is to know what real wear looks like, and also, to pick up a piece and see where your hands are most likely to touch.

Old varnish does not have a smooth surface, but has tiny craze or crackle marks through it. It does not look very shiny.

New varnish is often applied to something that was once painted, but has had its original paint sanded or stripped away. The texture is usually much glossier than old varnish. It is very difficult to remove old paint by either physical or chemical means without leaving some evidence on the woodenware. Wood is porous, and some pigment will remain in tiny, hard-to-clean pores. The end grain of wood in particular acts like a sponge. If the piece has been sanded without mercy to remove most traces of paint, the evidence of sanding itself is a telltale sign. Crisp, squared edges will be mushy and rounded. You will see tiny parallel lines from sandpaper or steel wool. Scribe marks, which are good places to check for traces of original paint, may be half eradicated by sanding. Don't hesitate to sniff the object. New paint and varnish retain their odors for quite some time.

Note that the phrase "original paint" and "old paint" do not necessarily mean the same thing. The same goes for varnish. "Original" means the first and only finish the object has had. "Old" usually means that it's been on a long time, but it's not what the maker did. An "old refinish" is not as good as original, but it's not bad, either. It means that the piece was refinished so long ago — fifty, seventy-five, or one hundred years — that the change in finish is by now itself an acceptable part of the piece's history. Many collectors and antiquarians in the early-to-mid-20th century refinished things to "improve" them. In the same spirit, some Shakers refinished furniture and interior woodwork at the same time.

Some woodenware never had a finish. Old unfinished wood in its original "as made" condition should look and feel dry. Although it may at first strike your eye as greatly in need of oil, wax, or polish, please refrain! It only takes a few minutes to forever change an original surface, and you will be hurting not only its aesthetic and historical value, but its dollar value as well. You can always see and/or feel the effects of oil, wax, or polish.

Exposure to light darkens wood, so most old unfinished wood has turned a rich, deep brown. It is very difficult to achieve this look with a stain.

5. If I don't have much money, can I still get something good?
Yes. If you have several hundred dollars, and you're patient and have a little luck, you can find something good to excellent in its category. Unpainted oval boxes are relatively low priced because painted boxes are so much in vogue. If you find one in good condition with its original surface, it will be good to excellent in its category, and it's not likely to be terribly expensive.

6. What should I *not* buy?
There are four categories of woodenware that we would not buy: things that are genuinely old, but not Shaker; Shaker reproductions whose finishes are faked to look old; outright fakes; and things that are genuinely Shaker, but have too many problems: refinished, replaced or missing parts, serious damage.

Old but not Shaker woodenware objects are the biggest category of things that we would not buy, and the main reason we have written this book. Objects in this category include:

a. Oval boxes with a single large finger on the body. The finger on the lid typically points in the opposite direction. These are commonly called "Harvard Shaker" boxes, but we have yet to learn why they are said to have been made by the Shakers in Harvard, Massachusetts. We have seen one such box that a reputable source said came from the Harvard Shakers, whose community closed in 1918. Even so, that's not enough evidence that these single-finger boxes were Shaker-made. Most of them are crude in comparison to Shaker oval boxes. We have never seen a Shaker box on which the lid and body fingers point in opposite directions.

b. Small 3-to-6-inch-high toylike pails with brightly painted exteriors. The interiors are often shiny white, and the hoops are usually painted black. The iron hoops, wire bails, and usually diamond-shaped bail plates are made of very flimsy stock. We have seen no evidence that these were made by the Shakers, and their quick, careless construction is not like the hundreds of genuine Shaker pails we've examined. We would especially not buy the decorated versions of these pails, with stenciled stars and phrases like "Good Boy," and in fact, we don't understand how such vividly ornamented items were ever attributed to the Shakers, who shunned decoration.

c. Heavy dippers with pointy handles. In the 19th century, New England's streams and rivers powered thousands of mills, many of which made pails, dippers, measures, and various other items. Frye's Measure Mill in Wilton, New Hampshire continues to produce "old-timey" wooden products. Check their mail-order catalogue for modern versions of old non-Shaker dippers.

d. Pails, tubs, or any coopered item with interlocking wooden hoops. Yes, the Shakers at New Lebanon, New York, and Hancock, Massachusetts, did use this construction technique in pails made in the first third of the 19th century. But that hardly means they made everything with this feature. The vast majority of woodenware items that we've seen with interlocking hoops have no association with the Shakers.

e. Round "pantry" boxes with straight seams. Yes, there are a handful of such boxes in museum collections that we know for sure are Shaker-made. But the form is so rare in documented Shaker examples that the chances of finding a genuine straight-seamed round box are very,

60. Miniature Firkin

Mid-19th century
Height: 2 ³/₈ inches
Diameter, bottom: 2 ³/₈ inches
Pine staves and bottom, hardwood
handle and hoops, yellow stain,
iron tacks
Philadelphia Museum of Art,
Gift of Mr. and Mrs. Julius Zieget

This miniature firkin is a good example of woodenware with excellent provenance that still may not be Shaker. It was acquired directly from Sister Marguerite Frost (1892-1971) of Canterbury, New Hampshire, with a handwritten note preserving the Shakers' oral tradition that it had been made by Brother Elijah Brown (1772-1851).

However, in spite of all this evidence, it is now thought to have been purchased, rather than made, by the Shakers in the mid-19th century. It is

possibly the work of the Hersey family in Hingham, Massachusetts.

The firkin was published as Shaker in *Shaker Design* (1986), and we have subsequently seen several similar examples sold as Shaker. But be aware that any information in print may have been updated since publication. Don't hesitate to check with the author of any book. The reference department of your library can give you the publisher's address, and publishers will forward letters to authors.

---

very slim. The quick-and-dirty workmanship on most pantry boxes alone should tell your eye, "no way" — poor-quality pine bottom and lid; flimsy, thin wood sides; few, crooked and widely spaced tacks; and a seam that has consequently rippled and buckled. A word here about the quality of Shaker work. It's not so much that other laborers did poor work as that they did ordinary work, while the Shakers characteristically put in extraordinary effort. The pantry boxes non-Shakers made were more than adequate for their purposes. Who cared very much about how they would hold up more than 150 years later? They were not made to last for centuries because that's not something the makers or users particularly cared about. The Shakers, who believed the millennium had come, were conscious of building their material world to endure for a long, long time.

61. **Oval Box**

Hingham, Massachusetts
Early to mid-19th century
Height: 1 ⁷/₈ inches
Length: 3 ⁵/₈ inches
Width: 2 ⁵/₈ inches
Pine lid and bottom, maple sides,
copper tacks and points
Collection of Ed Sawyer

We frequently see oval boxes with single large fingers called "Harvard Shaker" on the markets. But we have not seen proof that any such boxes were made by the Shakers in Harvard, Massachusetts, or anywhere else. Neither have we seen a Shaker box on which the lid and side fingers point in opposite directions. The poor workmanship on most similar boxes suggests instead that they are not Shaker.

This small box is relatively well made, of the same materials that the Shakers used — maple sides, pine top and bottom, copper tacks — but it is not a Shaker box. Inside the lid is an old paper label that shows that this box was made by Samuel Hersey of Hingham, Massachusetts. An inscription on the bottom indicates that it was a gift from a J.S. Lowell to L.C. Russell in 1867.

There are a few other differences. There are only four tiny copper tacks, or points, fastening the bottom to the box. Shaker boxes have more points. The oval is more rectangular than Shaker ovals. The inside seam is not fastened on the inside with a tack at the upper corner.

The box has darkened naturally over time but has never had a finish of any kind.

---

f. Churns. We have seen many churns on the market, and some are called Shaker, but we have not yet seen a churn that we can be certain is Shaker in a museum or private collection. The Shakers produced butter in such large quantities that it's unlikely they needed or used the small, standard household churn.

g. Firkins. Yes, we have seen a very few firkins that we believe are Shaker-made, but on the whole, you'd be unwise to pay a lot of money for a firkin of ordinary quality because it's very unlikely to be Shaker.

Reproductions with finishes altered to look old are also a problem, mostly with oval boxes. It's hard to make unfinished wood or new varnish look convincingly old, so the attempt is usually made with paint. There are thousands of reproduction oval boxes and carriers around. The less-well-made boxes would fool only the most naive of buyers, because their construction is clunky. However, a few craftspeople are making boxes of such high quality that they can fool even more experienced collectors. We have actually seen the lovely miniature oval boxes made by Northern Swallowtails offered at auction, smeared with paint and wiped to look worn. They didn't seem to fool anybody too much because they sold for a very low price, but be aware that this is happening.

Get to know what the best reproductions look like and who makes them. Some of the best oval box makers are Jerry Grant, now assistant director for collections at the Shaker Museum at Old Chatham, New York, and formerly box maker at Hancock Shaker Village; D. Clifford Myers, Hancock's current resident box maker; John Wilson of Charlotte, Michigan; and Eric Taylor and Betty Grondin of Northern Swallowtails, Danbury, New Hampshire. These makers sign their work to prevent fraud, but marks can be sanded away. If you see an obviously sanded spot, or feel an odd depression on the underside of the lid or on the bottom, be suspicious.

A few years ago, a very fine reproduction made Shaker auction history because it fooled a lot of people until one savvy collector blew the whistle on it. It was a small, delicate, rectangular carrier, made by Joel Seaman of Canaan, New York, formerly resident cabinetmaker at Hancock Shaker Village. It was stamped "JS" with a metal stamp and not really even altered to look old.

Part of the reason that the carrier could be passed as an original was the fact that genuinely old Shaker things can be in like-new condition if they were lightly used or not used at all. The Shakers tended to use things very carefully because everything belonged to the community and was intended to be passed along and used by succeeding generations of converts. Sometimes the reverse problem happens — someone will think a genuinely old Shaker object is a fake because it looks too clean and new. That's why it's vital to learn the provenance, if possible.

To date, we don't think you have to worry about reproductions of sieves, pails, or tubs. Remember, people who make reproductions are in business. They won't make something that has no market or that takes too much work for the return. Who in their right mind would perfect the art of sieve-making? Good-quality reproduction dippers are now being made by Bruce Graham of Harrodsburg, Kentucky. We have seen bad reproductions smeared with paint and wiped or sanded to look old — notably, some clunky modern dippers stained yellow and offered at auction.

There are a very few high-quality reproduction Shaker pails in existence made by Roger Gibbs of Concord, New Hampshire, and Ron Raiselis, cooper at Strawbery Banke, Portsmouth, New Hampshire, and formerly cooper at Old Sturbridge Village.

In general, to avoid being fooled by a doctored reproduction, look first at the form, then at the finish. Is the workmanship really as fine as the examples pictured in this book? Do all the parts really match in shape and proportions? If not — let it go. If the workmanship really is as good, then is the time to check the finish for genuine signs of age.

Out-and-out fakes are also beginning to appear in the Shaker woodenware market. We recently saw a small oval box with an "old red" stain that simply didn't look right. The top and bottom were clearly made of old wood, but the construction wasn't as good as it should have been. Jerry Grant confirmed that it was a fairly sophisticated fake. Alas, there are enough old boards around to provide plenty of new "old" lids and bottoms. Use common sense. It pays a faker to fake the most desirable and most valuable forms. Small oval boxes in paint fit this category more than anything else.

There is one more kind of fraud that we want to mention. That is the faked provenance. It's the easiest thing in the world for someone to look you in the eye and say, "Oh, yes, that piece came directly from the Shakers in 1942 to an old lady who sold it to me." The objects in question are usually genuinely old and simple, but not Shaker. We have seen and heard the silliest things. One dealer said a wool blanket came from "Sister Sara Lee" of the community in New Lebanon, New York. An auctioneer of dubious distinction told us that something came from "the niece" of Faith Andrews, the well-known authority and collector.

Here is where you have to know and trust the vendor. Luckily, the grapevine usually knows who's believable and who isn't. Just ask around a lot and you'll soon learn the kind of reputation a vendor has earned for himself or herself.

7. How can I take care of my woodenware?

This answer is simple: leave it alone. The perfect antique is something that was made and then just got old, without any changes except those made by time. We feel very strongly that just because someone has the money to buy an antique, he or she does not have the right to mistreat it. These things will outlast us. We like best the attitude of collectors who know that they are really temporary stewards of their things, whose

62. Firkin

Early 19th century
Height to rim: 9 ¹/₂ inches
Height including handle: 13 ¹/₂ inches
Diameter, top: 8 ¹/₄ inches
Diameter, bottom: 9 inches
Pine staves, lid, and bottom,
ash hoops and lid rim,
iron handles and tacks
Collection of Ed Sawyer

This unusual firkin is the only one we have seen with wrought-iron handles. The delicate handle is fastened on the inside with octagonal hand-cut iron nuts. Also odd are the two fingers on the lid.

The firkin form itself and the one-of-a-kind details would ordinarily cause us to hesitate to call this Shaker. However, it has an excellent provenance. Edward Deming Andrews included it in *The Community Industries of the Shakers* (1932) on page 143, identified as an "apple sauce bucket." It was published again posthumously in *Religion in Wood* (1966), on page 33, where his wife, Faith, called it a "sugar bucket."

The photos show that the missing hoop at the bottom has been gone for a long time. The firkin retains its original salmon-orange paint. It has faded, but the very bright original color remains visible on the side under the lid rim, where it has been protected from light. The bottom is not painted, which is unusual.

At this point, however, the collector needs to remember that a solid provenance and publication history do not make a piece Shaker.

The construction details do not relate to other products known to have been made by the Shakers. We cannot look at the handle for clues of Shaker manufacture since it is wrought iron. The wooden interlocking hoops are commonly found on non-Shaker coopered products. There are two rudimentary "fingers" on the rim of the lid, but these are much cruder than we expect to see on a product that is Shaker-made. An old repair made to the top hoop is not particularly well done.

Although the provenance is top-notch, we cannot say for sure that this particular firkin is Shaker-made. Like many other pieces of woodenware, it may have been purchased by the Shakers for use in the community, and it has become "Shaker" by association.

One of the features we love to see on unpainted oval boxes in original finish is the lovely, mellow, time-darkened color of the maple sides caused by exposure to light. This natural patina is almost impossible to duplicate with artificial staining. Like the skin on your hands, which darkens irregularly as you age, wood, too, develops "age spots" and a wide range of subtle variations in tone. Brown stain out of a can cannot achieve these variations. See, too, how the maple retains its original pale color at the rim where the lid shaded it from sunlight. Boxes in original finish will also be pale on the inside for the same reasons. We have seen more than a few boxes with dark stain on the insides, which we suppose are meant to look "aged." Don't be fooled. Most boxes are exceptionally clean on the insides. Remember, oval boxes held anything but liquids. Any coloring that looks like it was wet at some time is not original or from some old usage.

Note, too, how the pine top of the lid is generally the darkest wood on the whole box. Of course! A hundred and fifty years' worth of dust has fallen on the top, not on the sides.

responsibility is to keep the things protected for the next generation.

To add wax, oil, or polish is to change and damage the piece. To scrub it is just as bad. To refinish something is the ultimate foolish move. Our guideline: If it comes off with a soft brush, it's "dirt." If it doesn't, it's "patina." Some collectors use a very, very diluted solution of Murphy's Oil Soap in warm water with a soft, well-wrung-out sponge and wipe very gently to remove surface dirt. We feel reluctant to suggest this because it's too easy to use too heavy a hand. Remember, water can raise the grain of wood permanently. If the thing is just too crummy to give you pleasure, why buy it?

A tip for pails and tubs: since wood dries out in heated rooms in winter, consider storing your pails upside down. That way the hoops can't fall down and leave you with a pile of staves to fit back together.

8. What else can I do to be a wise collector?

We know many, many collectors. The list that follows summarizes what we have learned from them.

a. The best collectors are patient. They never, never impulse-buy just because they "have to buy something" right now, today. That's compulsion, not collecting. That leads you to see Shaker where it isn't or to overlook problems like damage or a wrong finish. If you want a Shaker box or pail, you'll find a good one sooner or later.

b. The best collectors buy the best examples they can afford. They won't buy a "bargain" because it has a defect that makes it more affordable. They would rather have an unpainted oval box in a less desirable midsize in excellent condition than a painted oval box with a replaced lid, cracks, or all the other possible problems.

c. The best collectors catalogue what they own. That is, they make a note of what they bought, where and when, how much they paid, and — most important — what they know of the piece's history, tracing the piece back, if possible, to when it left a Shaker community. They write this information down and photograph the piece so that someone else would know exactly what they know if they were hit by a truck tomorrow. In so doing, they preserve the piece's provenance and can greatly enhance its dollar value.

d. The best collectors look very carefully and very slowly. They ask to take the piece out into the daylight to examine it inch by inch. (Daylight is the only light in which to look at finishes.) They don't often miss a very fine repair or replaced part or anything else that would be an unpleasant surprise later, at home.

63. "M-y Kitchen" Firkin

South Hingham, Massachusetts
Mid-19th century
Height to lid: 9 ³/₄ inches
Diameter, bottom: 10 inches
Pine staves and bottom,
ash handle and hoops, teal paint,
large round-headed copper tacks
Collection of Ed Sawyer

This firkin in teal blue paint is a good example of woodenware that was owned by the Shakers, but not made by them. Its provenance is excellent. It was purchased by the present owners from Faith Andrews, well known with her husband, Edward Deming Andrews, as an early Shaker collector and scholar. The Andrewses had acquired it directly from one of the surviving Shaker communities sometime between the late 1920s and the 1950s.

Apart from its provenance, the painted inscription on the front — "M-y Kitchen." — is a clue to Shaker use. The letters M and Y together appear on other Shaker things and may be an abbreviation for Ministry. The Shakers commonly marked small, portable objects to make sure they were put back where they belonged, a practice that made sense where everything was communally owned and where order was important.

However, the lid is clearly stamped with the name of a worldly maker: "C. & A. WILDER/SO. HINGHAM/ MASS." The Shakers made and sold lots of products, including woodenware, but they also bought when it was practical to do so. This firkin is of interest as an example of what the Shakers thought suitable to buy. But a collector would want to be aware that this is not an example of the Shakers' own work. For more information on Shaker firkins, see page 134.

---

e. The best collectors are humble, inquisitive, and intelligent. They aren't too proud to ask questions and they don't assume they know all there is to know. They know who the authorities are in any given specialized subject area and they don't hesitate to contact those authorities with questions. They read, attend forums and conferences, and make themselves known to museum curators who enjoy their company and who inevitably learn from them, too.

f.   The best collectors have built-in alarm systems that go off when they hear something described as "unique." They know this means that there are no other documented examples with which to compare the object. They know that the term "unique" is often used with things that are old but not Shaker. Unscrupulous vendors know that "unique" makes the buyer feel important because he or she owns the "only" one in existence. They know enough to understand that unless the object has parts that unquestionably relate to other known Shaker items (for instance, on page 62, the round carrier's fingers and handle), they may well make a mistake.

SHAKER COMMUNITIES

CHRONOLOGY

BIBLIOGRAPHY

INDEX

SHAKER COMMUNITIES THEN AND NOW

**	1	New Lebanon, New York	(1787-1947)
**	2	Watervliet, New York	(1787-1938)
***	3	Enfield, Connecticut	(1790-1917)
**	4	Hancock, Massachusetts	(1790-1960)
***	5	Harvard, Massachusetts	(1791-1918)
*	6	Canterbury, New Hampshire	(1792-present)
***	7	Tyringham, Massachusetts	(1792-1875)
***	8	Alfred, Maine	(1793-1931)
**	9	Enfield, New Hampshire	(1793-1923)
***	10	Shirley, Massachusetts	(1793-1908)
*	11	Sabbathday Lake, Maine	(1794-present)
**	12	Pleasant Hill, Kentucky	(1814-1910)
**	13	Union Village, Ohio	(1812-1910)
***	14	Watervliet, Ohio	(1806-1900)
***	15	South Union, Kentucky	(1807-1922)
***	16	Gorham, Maine	(1808-1819)
***	17	West Union, Indiana	(1810-1827)
***	18	Savoy, Massachusetts	(1817-1825)
***	19	North Union, Ohio	(1822-1889)
***	20	Whitewater, Ohio	(1824-1907)
***	21	Sodus, New York	(1826-1936)
***	22	Groveland, New York	(1836-1892)
***	23	Narcoossee, Florida	(1896-1911)
***	24	White Oak, Georgia	(1898-1902)

CHRONOLOGY OF IMPORTANT DATES

1736	Ann Lee is born in Manchester, England.
1758	Ann Lee joins the "Shaking Quakers."
1774	Ann Lee and eight followers come to America.
1776	First Shaker settlement at Niskayuna, New York.
1780	The Shakers "open the gospel" and seek converts; Joseph Meacham joins the Shakers.
1784	Mother Ann dies.
1785	First meetinghouse built at New Lebanon, New York.
1794	By this date eleven villages established "in gospel order."
1805	Three Shaker missionaries travel to Kentucky.
1806	First western society established at Pleasant Hill, Kentucky.

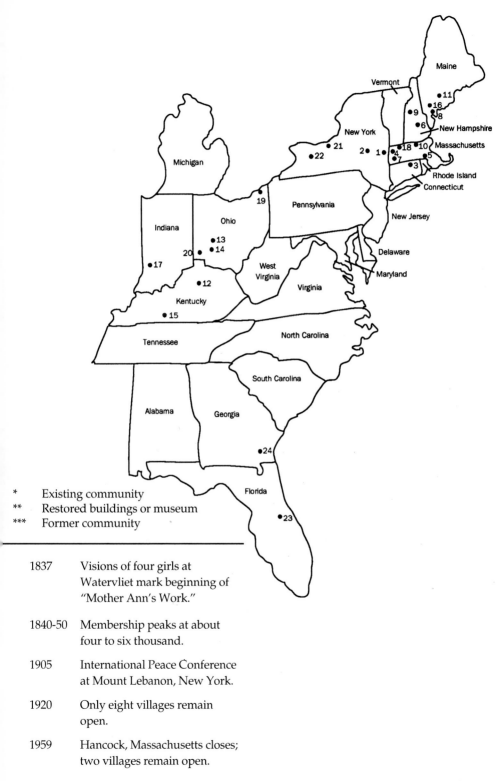

*   Existing community
**   Restored buildings or museum
*** Former community

1837	Visions of four girls at Watervliet mark beginning of "Mother Ann's Work."
1840-50	Membership peaks at about four to six thousand.
1905	International Peace Conference at Mount Lebanon, New York.
1920	Only eight villages remain open.
1959	Hancock, Massachusetts closes; two villages remain open.

SELECTED BIBLIOGRAPHY

Andrews, Edward Deming. *The Community Industries of the Shakers.* Albany: The University of the State of New York, 1932.

_____. *The People Called Shakers: A Search for the Perfect Society.* New York: Oxford University Press, 1953.

Andrews, Edward Deming, and Faith Andrews. *Religion in Wood: A Book of Shaker Furniture.* Bloomington: Indiana University Press, 1966.

_____. *Shaker Furniture: The Craftsmanship of an American Communal Sect.* New Haven, Connecticut. Yale University Press, 1937.

_____. *Fruits of the Shaker Tree of Life: Memoirs of Fifty Years of Collecting and Research.* Stockbridge, Massachusetts: The Berkshire Traveller Press, 1975.

Butler, Linda, and June Sprigg. *Inner Light: The Shaker Legacy.* New York: Alfred A. Knopf, 1985.

Gould, Mary Earle. *Early American Wooden Ware.* rev. ed. Springfield, Massachusetts: The Pond-Ekberg Company, 1948.

Handberg, Ejner. *Measured Drawings of Shaker Furniture and Woodenware.* Stockbridge, Massachusetts: The Berkshire Traveller Press, 1980.

_____. *Shop Drawings of Shaker Furniture and Woodenware, Volume I.* Stockbridge, Massachusetts: The Berkshire Traveller Press, 1973.

_____. *Shop Drawings of Shaker Furniture and Woodenware, Volume II.* Stockbridge, Massachusetts: The Berkshire Traveller Press, 1975.

_____. *Shop Drawings of Shaker Furniture and Woodenware, Volume III.* Stockbridge, Massachusetts: The Berkshire Traveller Press, 1977.

Kassay, John. *The Book of Shaker Furniture.* Amherst: The University of Massachusetts Press, 1980.

Klamkin, Marian. *The Collector's Book of Boxes.* New York: Dodd, Mead & Co., 1970.

_____. *Hands to Work: Shaker Folk Art and Industries.* New York: Dodd, Mead & Company, 1972.

Little, Nina Fletcher. *Neat and Tidy.* New York: Dutton, 1978.

Meader, Robert F.W. *Illustrated Guide to Shaker Furniture.* New York: Dover Publications, 1972.

Morse, Flo. *The Shakers and the World's People.* New York: Dodd, Mead & Company, 1980.

New York State Museum, Albany. *Community Industries of the Shakers: A New Look.* (Exhibition catalogue), 1983.

Pinto, Edward H. *Treen or Small Woodenware Throughout the Ages.* London, New York, Toronto, Sydney: B.T. Batsford, Ltd., 1949.

Rieman, Timothy D., and Charles R. Muller. *The Shaker Chair.* Canal Winchester, Ohio: The Canal Press, 1984.

Rose, Milton C., and Emily Mason Rose, eds. *A Shaker Reader.* New York: Universe Books, 1977.

Shea, John G. *The American Shakers and Their Furniture.* New York: Van Nostrand, 1971.

Sprigg, June. *By Shaker Hands.* New York: Alfred A. Knopf, 1975.

_____. *Shaker Design.* New York: Whitney Museum of American Art in association with W.W. Norton & Co., 1986.

_____. *Shaker Life, Work, and Art.* New York: Stewart, Tabori & Chang, Inc., 1987.

_____. "Marked Shaker Furnishings." *Antiques,* May 1979, pp. 1048-58.

_____. *Shaker: Masterworks of Utilitarian Design Created between 1800 and 1875.* Katonah, New York: The Katonah Gallery, 1983.

_____. "Shaker Oval Boxes." Catalogue: 1985 Antiques Show. Philadelphia: University of Pennsylvania Hospital, 1985.

_____. "Shaker Perfection." *Art and Antiques,* June 1985, pp. 58-63.

INDEX

ABOUT THE AUTHORS

June Sprigg studied early American culture and material culture in the Winterthur Museum graduate program. She is currently Curator of Collections at Hancock Shaker Village in Pittsfield, Massachusetts. She is the author of many articles and books on the Shakers, including *Shaker: Life, Work, and Art*. She was curator of the 1986 landmark exhibit, "Shaker Design" at the Whitney Museum of American Art.

Jim Johnson is a partner in a marketing firm in Lee, Massachusetts, and a consultant and dealer in Shaker antiques. He is co-author with June Sprigg of *Colonial Design in the New World*.

Principal photographer Paul Rocheleau has been published in numerous magazines, including *Antiques Magazine, Antiques World, Americana, American Craft,* and *Architectural Digest*. His photography was featured in the catalogue of the 1986 exhibit, "Shaker Design," at the Whitney Museum of American Art. His books include *Shaker Design, O Appalachia,* and the New England editions of the *Smithsonian Guide to Historic America*.

Design: Werner Mischke
Composition: Graphic Innovations
Typeface: Palatino
Printing: R.R. Donnelley